MASTER YOUR MINDSET

MASTER YOUR MINDSET

Live a Meaningful Life

MICHAEL PILARCZYK

WILEY

Published by John Wiley & Sons, Inc., Hoboken, New Jersey.
Published simultaneously in Canada.

Editors: Sjors Sommer and Jet Hopser

US Editor: Julie Kerr

Translation: Jackie Davis and Michael Pilarczyk

For general information on our other products and services or for technical support, please contact our Customer Care Department within the United States at (800) 762-2974, outside the United States at (317) 572-3993 or fax (317) 572-4002.

Wiley also publishes its books in a variety of electronic formats. Some content that appears in print may not be available in electronic formats. For more information about Wiley products, visit our web site at www.wiley.com.

Library of Congress Control Number: 2025900582

ISBN: 9781394320127 (cloth)

ISBN: 9781394320134 (ePub)

ISBN: 9781394320141 (ePDF)

Cover Design: Wiley

SKY10097971_020725

The book you now have in your hands is like a shovel that you can use to dig within yourself. You'll discover answers and insights that will give you guidance on where you want to go in your life. You can unearth all the truths about yourself if you're willing to dig deep into the mine of your own soul. If you do, you'll discover that you are the creator of your own character and the designer of your own destiny.

—Michael George Pilarczyk

Contents

Author Note

This book is intended to help you reach your maximum potential and make a positive difference in the world. We cannot give you any guarantees of the results. We do not believe in programs and books that promise wealth, success, happiness, or enlightenment in a short time. These can only be achieved through hard and smart work, a well-founded strategic plan, delivering unique added value, perseverance, and serving others with your talents and quality services. Any action you take related to the contents of this book is your own responsibility. Decisions based on the contents of this book are made voluntarily. We advise you to consult your specialists before you undertake any drastic actions that can have consequences of any nature whatsoever. Under no circumstances will the author and publisher be held liable for any consequences and/or results arising from the use of this book. We wish you success and happiness.

Live your best life!

*"I am the master of my faith
The captain of my soul."*

—*William Ernest Henley*, Invictus

*"A beautiful, healthy, wealthy, and successful life
is possible for so many people, if only there was access
to the right insights, key knowledge, good role models,
and extraordinary teachers to learn from."*

Introduction

This Book Can Change Your Life

How WOULD YOU like to live your ideal life? A meaningful life, whatever that may look like to you personally. To paint a clearer picture of that, I wrote this book for you.

Can one book change your life? Absolutely. With me that was certainly the case. The book was *Think and Grow Rich* by Napoleon Hill. I was 21 the first time I read it, and it became the foundation for the way I live. Since then, I've been fortunate enough to become a renowned DJ, TV host, successful businessman, world sailor, meditation teacher, inspirational speaker, and bestselling author.

Yes, I've been very fortunate to make all my dreams come true, and I'm very grateful for that. But success never comes without setbacks, disappointments, and deep lows. Sometimes life takes you on a bumpy ride and tries to knock you down. But for those who pass that mental test and refuse to give up, life offers a fair reward. For me, that reward was financial freedom at the age of 37.

A beautiful, healthy, wealthy, and successful life is possible for so many people, if only there was access to the right insights, key knowledge, good role models, and extraordinary teachers to learn from. I know from experience that I can be that person, helping you live your best life. How do I know that? Well, I am living my best life. I'm 55 now. I've been through a lot and I have learned a lot. But most importantly, I practice what I preach.

Here's an important piece of advice to remember: if someone wants to show you the way, first ask if they've walked that path themselves. Never just take someone's word for it. Always ask yourself if that person has the right to speak on the matter. What have they accomplished themselves?

Now, you may be thinking, "Yeah, that's easy for you to say, but such a rich and luxurious life isn't in the cards for everyone." And maybe it's not for everyone—but not everyone will read this book. You, however, are reading it. So, what's on your wish list? Happiness, money, personal growth? Your dream home with the love of your life? More free time, a trip around the world, your own business, living on the beach or in the quiet mountains? More peace of mind? What does your best life look like? Have you ever seriously thought about that? And more importantly, have you written down that wish list in concrete terms?

In this book, I'll ask a lot of questions—because questions are more important than answers. Questions make you think, and thinking leads to insights. Why do you do what you do? Why do you think the way you do? And how do you know if your thoughts align with the life you truly want to live? If you pay close attention while reading this book, the answers will arise within you.

This isn't a theoretical self-help book. I don't believe in programs or books that promise quick success, instant wealth, or enlightenment. Nor do I believe you have to be a millionaire to live your best life—though having money is practical. Money can help you achieve your goals and create the lifestyle you desire, but it's not the whole picture.

Much of this book is about awareness. Getting to the bottom of yourself so that you understand what causes your thinking and your behavior. This will give you peace of mind and also the power to start living life the way you want. You will be less likely to lose yourself in emotions that determine your behavior, and you will spend much less time brooding. On the contrary, you will become much more decisive in the choices you make, and you will gain more control over your behavior and thus over your daily life. And only when you know yourself are you able to understand how other people think and able to explain their behavior. This makes your dealings with others easier, and you will find that, as a result, many obstacles you're faced with and resistance you face will disappear from your life. It paves the way to start living your life the way you would prefer. A meaningful life.

Master Your Mindset is based on the *Think and Grow Rich* principles, to which I have added my own unique experiences in life and business, and all the valuable lessons I've learned from my teachers, including my business mentor, Mr. Dan Peña.

I share with you my personal story. How I, by trial and error, made my dreams come true, found inner peace, and achieved freedom, both spiritually and financially. Is this what you want too? Then you'll find questions and answers in this book that will help you on your way. I share what I've done and how I've done it. And how you can apply the same way of thinking and the same strategy to improve the quality of your own life.

Don't expect your life to suddenly look completely different tomorrow. That requires more than simply reading this book. You have to study it and live it. I will help you along the way, and I will explain to you in detail what you have to do. I'll guide you through it, you'll reflect on it, and ultimately, you'll decide what to do with it. But it's also important to know that without action there will be no results.

You can't change your life in a day, but you can change your daily life. The secret of long-lasting success is found in your daily routine. Gold and diamonds are only found by searching and digging. The book you now have in your hands is like a shovel that you can use to dig within yourself. You'll discover answers and insights that will give you guidance on where you want to go in your life. You can unearth all the truths about yourself if you're willing to dig deep into the mine of your own soul. If you do, you'll discover that you are the creator of your own character and the maker of your own destiny.

> *"Life is an adventure waiting to be taken on,*
> *a mystery to discover, an opportunity to seize,*
> *a challenge to take up.*
> *Life is both the journey and the destination.*
> *Life is so beautiful.*
> *Wake up, live."*

What Does Your Best Life Look Like?

This might not be an easy question. It's a big question. And to understand big things, it's best to break it down into manageable chunks. You don't need to be able to answer that question in detail yet.

To begin with: What would you like to change in your daily life? Why aren't you doing more of what you would like to be doing? And why do you do things even though you'd rather not? After we explore these questions, I'll take you through more philosophical questions. Why do you get out of bed every day? Why do you do what you do? What do you do it all for? Finally, the last questions, and not the easiest ones: Who are you really, deep down? And who do you want to be?

This book is about these essential life questions.

I've asked thousands of people these questions. Virtually no one has been able to give clear and concrete answers to them. Yet their importance has become increasingly clear to me. They make you think; they bring insights. They awaken your consciousness. Both the questions and the many different answers to them remind me of Apple founder Steve Jobs' legendary words at Stanford University in 2005: "Your time is limited, so don't waste it by living someone else's life. Don't be trapped by dogma—which is living with the results of other people's thinking. Don't let the noise of other people's opinions drown out your own inner voice. And most importantly, have the courage to follow your heart and intuition. They somehow know what you genuinely want."

To live your best life, you first have to master your mindset, master the way you think. That way of thinking determines your vision of the world around you and of yourself, your self-image. Using countless examples and my own experiences, I'll help you understand your way of thinking: how it came to be and the unseen blockages that might now be preventing you from living your best life.

Do you feel like you're not yet making use of your full personal potential, that there's more to you? Do you have goals you want to achieve? Do you have dreams you want to make come true? Do you want to give deeper meaning to who you are and what you do?

The examples I use in this book will show how your thoughts guide your behavior. And that your behavior determines both your daily actions and the results you get. It all starts with the way you think.

It's important to be aware of your thoughts and of the fact that you are the cause of that mental activity. Realize that you assign meaning to every thought with that intelligent brain of yours. And that through infusing thoughts with meaning, you give rise to certain feelings and emotions. Additionally, every judgment you have is also the result of the meaning you assign to your thoughts. Reading this book now, you're forming thoughts about it—you have an opinion on it. You might agree or disagree with what I have to say. Where does that opinion come from?

Over the years and while I was doing research for this book, it became clear to me how the way we think comes about. It's the result of our perception, and our perception isn't an objective representation of reality. It's the lens through which you see life. It's your personal reality. Not pure, therefore, but colored. "Reality is merely an illusion, albeit a very persistent one," claimed Albert Einstein.

Watching a film is a good example of how your perception determines your reality. Despite the fact that you know what is on screen isn't real, you can have a sleepless night after watching an exciting thriller or a gripping drama. And how many times have you not shed a tear or two when watching an especially heartbreaking death scene? Your thoughts and emotions can, therefore, make you believe in something that resembles reality yet is actually made up.

Something similar happens when you watch an illusionist. You know beforehand that what you're going to see isn't real, but still, you believe in that temporary illusion. Things don't only work that way when you're watching a movie or an illusionist. It's also how you look at the outside world. You experience it as reality through your perception, and through the personal lenses of your conditioning.

Your experience of reality is affected by everything that filters through the lens of your perception. Day in, day out, you're programmed by what you see and read: the news. But is all that news true? Is everything you see really real? In recent years, we've heard the term "fake news" bandied about, but what is that, really? And who decides what's true and what isn't? Some people are convinced that something is true "because it was on the news." Still others don't believe everything just because someone said so and do their own research into "the truth." In this way, everyone chooses their own truth to believe in.

One final example: Just like you use a filter to edit photos on Instagram to make them more beautiful, you view the outside world through your own filter. And that filter colors things the way you want to see them. This is called a paradigm: a frame of reference from which you interpret reality. Your convictions are formed from that frame of reference. In this book, we're going to carefully investigate that filter. I want to show you the influence that filter has on your view of the world and on yourself. And vice versa: What influence do you have on your own filter?

Your filter is the consequence of your paradigms and conditioning; it's your way of thinking. And since you are the cause of your thoughts, you also have the ability and the opportunity to change those thoughts, and thereby change what you see and what you get in life.

The title of this book is *Master Your Mindset: Live a Meaningful Life.* Your mindset is your way of thinking, and it determines how you lead your life: whether you're happy and successful or not, how you interact with others and with yourself, how you deal with your feelings, and whether you live life the way you'd like. Your behavior is, therefore, a direct consequence of your mindset. Do you want to improve something about yourself, your behavior, and the quality of your daily life? Then you'll need to change your mindset and your convictions.

If you're 25 years old, you'll read this book differently than if you're 40 or 55. Where you're at on your life path largely determines how you'll interpret my words. The beauty of it is that everything I write is universal. It works for everyone, including you, provided you're open to it.

That's why I ask you to read this book with an open mind. Read receptively suspend your judgment. I have no intention to convince you of anything, so I'm not out to prove anything. I'm not a scientist. But I know what works based on my own experience and the results of the tens of thousands of people I've taught in recent years.

If you don't believe in what I have to tell you, it won't work for you. First believe, and then you'll see. That's my mantra.

There are four parts to this book. In the first part, I will tell you briefly about my life, where I got the knowledge and wisdom that have made me who I am now. It's my personal story, but if you read carefully, you'll discover you can use many elements of my philosophy and strategy to create your own best life.

In Part II, I describe that philosophy: the quest for happiness and success, for yourself, for your personal values, and for your own truth. This helps to form your personal statute: a guide with your own rules for life, which then determines the quality of your life. I want to mention right away that success and happiness are not an end unto their own. They are not a "place" you reach. Success and happiness are experienced when you live a certain way. They are a state of being, a way of life.

In Part III, you'll learn how to master your mindset, your thinking. If you know that your behavior, how you feel, and the results you get are the result of your thinking, then it's also critical to understand how your thinking mind works. I will explain the origins of your way of thinking and how you can transform self-limiting beliefs into a powerful, positive mindset.

In Part IV, I explain the strategy that underpins my own continued success. This part is about the path to success and happiness. But again, it's as much about the journey as the destination. It's your way of living that will bring you success and enable you to experience happiness. Using practical principles and examples, I explain how you can achieve your personal and business goals and make your dreams a reality. This requires a well-thought-out strategy, which I describe in my 12-step plan. I've developed this strategy and philosophy over the years, and it's grounded in my experiences as a human being and an entrepreneur. Moreover, I've also been inspired by many professionals and spiritual teachers. It's a philosophy that can be seen in the mindsets of sports heroes, famous artists, top entrepreneurs, and other successful people.

Perhaps what I'm writing is new to you and a whole world will open up as you read this book. Maybe what I have to share is already obvious to you. Perhaps you think you already know it all. But there is a vast difference between knowing and understanding. If you think you "already know it all" but your life still isn't what you'd like it to be, then you don't have it all figured out. Don't tell me that you know it, show it!

Understanding is doing what you know and doing it frequently. It sounds simple, but discipline and repetition lead to success. That's a universal principle. Spend as much time as possible studying and practicing. Only by taking action can you achieve the results you aim for.

What I'm telling you is derived from centuries-old wisdom. These insights have been passed on for generations. I've borrowed many of them from books and stories by Napoleon Hill, James Allen, George Clason, Wayne W. Dyer, Alan Watts, Jiddu Krishnamurti, Wallace D. Wattles, Tulku Lobsang Rinpoche, Sri Sri Ravi Shankar, Deepak Chopra, Bob Proctor, Richard Branson, Tony Robbins, and Jim Rohn. I've done my utmost to explore and understand their intentions, insights, and wisdom.

This—supplemented with what I've learned from my business mentor, Dan Peña; my spiritual teacher, Rajshree Patel; and my life coach, Egon Massink—has become my philosophy of life. I share that vision and mindset in this book so you, too, can apply it to live your best life.

"Belief in yourself is your greatest power."

Follow Your Desires

The recipe for a happy and successful life is simple: do what you really like, and become extremely good at it. That may sound like an oversimplification, but it's precisely this simplicity in thought and deed that characterizes many successful people.

Three decades ago, when I was 21, I wasn't consciously on a quest to understand how the mind works. I was more interested in how some were able to earn millions and lead lives of luxury while most others went to work every day, earning salaries that just paid the bills—the difference between making a life and making a living. If you're happy with that, that's wonderful, but I noticed that a lot of people were happy when the weekend came around again or when they could finally take a vacation. What does it say about your work when you're overjoyed that it's Friday afternoon? That it's time to leave your job and do something you do like!

Of course, I understand that bills have to be paid. You need to work to support yourself, but then why not do something that you like and that brings you satisfaction? If you don't enjoy your job, someone will pick up on that sooner or later, with the result that you'll have no other choice but to look for another job. And if you reluctantly go about your work, it just gobbles up your energy. It'll never make you happy, you'll never have the intention to get better at it, and you'll never perform beyond average.

When I was 37, I was ranked on a list of the hundred wealthiest self-made millionaires under 40, similar to Forbes 40 Under 40, with a stated net worth of $9 million. What made these people in their twenties and thirties multimillionaires so early in their lives? The vast majority of them were living for their passion. They worked with passion, they did what made them happy, and by spending all their time on it, they managed to achieve extraordinary things. The resulting fame, wealth, or both is a byproduct and hardly ever a goal unto itself. Many of these successful entrepreneurs, artists, and athletes don't hide the fact that the financial outcome of their activities is also a driving force. But it's usually not the predominant one.

Following your desires automatically points you in the right direction on your life path. This requires courage, trust, and faith in yourself. In *The Alchemist*, Paulo Coelho writes: "Remember that wherever your heart is, there you will find your treasure."

Not listening to your heart and ignoring your desires often leads to a dead end. That happened to a friend of mine from school named Chris. He didn't have to do much to get A's and B's, and classmates and teachers alike thought Chris was intelligent. We didn't really know what our fathers did for a living, except that they left early in the morning and came home late in the evening—and that all had to do with traffic jams. That was in the early 1980s, and we were in high school. Chris and I vowed we would never get stuck in traffic jams just to go work for a boss. We had dreams and futures rich with possibilities.

A few years ago, I went to our reunion. It was great to see the people I'd shared my life with so long ago, and we talked about how the past few decades had gone for everyone. For fun, I shouted out, "Who sits in traffic jams in the morning?" The room fell silent. All but one of them raised their hands, and it wasn't Chris. "I don't know what happened along the way," he later said. Things had gone differently than he'd wanted. "It was the circumstances at the time. I listened too much to people around me who thought I shouldn't do this and shouldn't do that. I wanted to make so many other choices. . ."

"Chris, why didn't you?" I asked him. He didn't know. "How old are you now?"

"Forty-three," he answered.

"What are you going to do with the rest of your life?"

And Chris thought about that question for a while. I found it fascinating. Two people with nearly identical backgrounds, who went to the same school, from the same kind of neighborhood—how could he, with all his intelligence, be unhappily trapped in his life while I was living my best life?

"All we have to do is decide what to do with the time given us."

– J.R.R. Tolkien, *The Lord of the Rings*

Your Life Has a Deadline

Suppose it were possible to redefine your existence. What would you want to do? What would you change? Would you dare to follow your heart and make your dreams come true?

You may think you have all the time in the world ahead of you. In reality, though, your future gets shorter every day. This life has a deadline, and although we all know this, we're often not really aware of it, especially when we're young. I'm not saying you have to entertain notions of your own mortality every day, but if you have greater appreciation for each moment, you'll show more gratitude, and gratitude is a form of happiness.

For that reason alone, it's good to consciously reflect on this. But let it also guide your actions, your choices. What would you do if you were told today that you had no more than one year left to live? Take time to think about this. What would you no longer do? What would you not spend a minute more on? And what would you do with those last few months? What decisions would you make right now? And why?

Suppose the day of your death was already determined on the day you were born. That would mean you'd know when your last day on this planet would be. Would this affect the way you live now? If so, how?

What have you done with your time? You need to take time to contemplate this question. What have you done with your time over the past few months, over the past 5 or 10 years? Where do you stand on your own timeline between birth and. . . the as-yet-unknown end? You don't know how much time you have left, but you do know the path you've traveled. What have you spent your time on? That has largely determined where you are now in your life. A very important question: What have you done with your time?

I often hear that we don't have enough time. Is that true? What would you do if you had more time available? "If I had more time, I could earn more money and do more fun things," someone said to me. "That's an illusion," I explained. "More time doesn't exist." I quoted the words of Gandalf the wizard from *The Lord of the Rings*: "All we have to do is decide what to do with the time that is given us."

Every day, you make choices. You choose to do certain things and not do others. This means you set priorities, either consciously or unconsciously. Why do you sometimes not do things you'd like or need to do, and instead waste your time on activities that don't contribute to your happiness and quality of life? It's of inestimable value to be in harmony with the choices you consciously make because then you can meaningfully spend the time you've been given. In our modern society, our life is governed by time and money. And money largely determines how we spend our time.

Dreams Are Seeds

"Dreams are the seeds of a future reality," Napoleon Hill wrote in *Think and Grow Rich*. Desire is the source of every success. Your soul's power assists you in making that deep desire a reality. Great explorers, inventors, sports heroes, artists, musicians, and successful entrepreneurs are all driven by a boundless desire. Genuine desire produces energy, miraculously making you one with the energy of the universe, which I call "Cosmic Intelligence." By this I mean energy, visualization, imagination, and the law of attraction and creation. We'll revisit these fundamental elements later in this book.

I'd like to ask you a few important life questions: What do you sometimes dream of? What would you really like? What do you do it all for? What does your best life look like?

To give worthwhile meaning to your life, it's important to transform your desires into concrete goals. Where are you heading if you have no idea what your destination is? Imagine you hop into your car and set your navigation device to "wherever." Where do you think you'll end up? If you don't know where you're going, there's a good chance you'll end up somewhere you don't want to be. It works the same way with your personal navigation system. Program your own destination. What end result do you want? Once that's clear, you can envision it. And if you can envision it, then there's almost always a way to get there. How you're going to get there isn't relevant at this point, but you have to know exactly where you want to go.

It's of absolute importance that you decide on a direction, just as a ship's captain sets course for the next destination. It doesn't have to be your final destination right away, so don't think that you should have one huge life purpose right off the bat. A goal can also be an in-between step in achieving your ultimate, bigger goals or making your dreams come true.

If you have a dream, it can literally determine the destination of your life. Sailing is something I dreamed of since I was little. I was six when my father took me out on a little rented wooden boat on a small lake. That afternoon gave birth to my longing to take long sailing trips and live on a boat, and that dream became my driving force. It took 30 years before I made it come true. The ones who hang in there win, maybe not every time, but often. Winners never quit, and quitters never win.

> "If you don't know where you're going, there's a good chance you'll end up somewhere you don't want to be."

Whatever You Can Conceive and Believe, You Can Achieve

Dreams give you the strength to change your life, and even the world. History has been largely written by creative people and dreamers. I'm not suggesting that everyone has to become a world champion or megastar.

Nor do I claim that everything is possible for everyone. That's not the case; every individual has their own personal potential. But don't immediately allow this to become a self-limiting thought.

Don't also think you can only have dreams when you're young or have exceptional talents. Or that making dreams come true is only for the lucky few. It's about whether you have the courage to dare to dream. My advice: follow your desire, listen to your heart, live with passion.

You have your own vision of life and how you want to lead yours. You have your own wishes, goals, and dreams. "Whatever the mind of man can conceive and believe, it can achieve," said Napoleon Hill in *Think and Grow Rich*.

Buddha tells us in his lessons that we're formed by our thoughts. We become what we think. I share that philosophy. I also believe that you're almost always able to do more than your rational mind can possibly imagine.

Whenever I talk about great role models who knew early on what their dreams or passions were, I often hear the refrain "Most people don't know exactly what they want; it's really hard, especially when you're young." This sounds to me like the kind of self-limiting thoughts that originate in our education. School doesn't educate us to lead successful and happy lives; rather, it gives us a false sense of security and prepares us for a job. Unfortunately, educational systems are trapped in webs of regulations and leave little room for innovation and creativity. At home and at school, they tell you what the rules are, but hardly anyone teaches you how to play the game. You learn that the lines are the limits, but who teaches you how to score?

I really like teaching and working with young people because I'm interested in how they see things. In my lectures at colleges and universities, I always ask students about their goals and dreams. That question often overwhelms them. They do not have a list of clear goals. Most students have never really thought deeply about their goals and dreams.

And when I ask what they think determines whether a person becomes successful and rich, I get remarkable answers: wealthy parents, you have to have to start off with money, you need to know the right people who can help you get a good job, and, above all, you shouldn't make many mistakes. I tell them mistakes make great teachers. By making lots of them, sometimes even painful ones, I've become who I am now and can live life the way I want to. See making mistakes as learning moments. By learning from them, you gain experience, and you become better at something.

Of course, it can certainly work to your advantage if you know the right people, yet if you don't offer added value, those people won't line up to hire you.

Many of the students I've spoken to think hard work and excellence aren't deciding factors for success. According to them, external factors over which they can't exert any influence determine the course of their lives. Where do these misleading convictions come from? Who put up these invisible prison bars?

If it's true that so many people can't figure out what they really want, why is that? What's the reason for it? Our upbringing? Our educational system compartmentalizes us and then expects us to make a choice for the rest of our lives within this limited range of possibilities.

> *"At home and at school, they tell you what*
> *the rules are, but hardly anyone teaches you*
> *how to play the game.*
> *You learn that the lines are the limits,*
> *but who teaches you how to score?"*

What School Doesn't Teach You

"How do I figure out what I like?" I hear it time and again. How can you not know? Or do you not dare to say it out loud? Perhaps because of fear? Because you're afraid that it's not possible, that you won't succeed? Are you afraid of being disappointed? Is that why you don't dare to dream of your most ideal life? In the past, when you were younger, your mind was still free. Your imagination fueled a vibrant existence. But time robs many people of their dreams. You allow your imagination to run dry and your creative ability to die off. Do you think that's how you avoid disappointment?

Is that why parents and teachers don't ask you to dream without limits? "You have to be realistic," they say. What's realistic? Thinking from within their limited thoughts? Because they themselves have never stepped up to the plate out of fear, or "because that's the way it's supposed to be," or because they were also robbed of their own dreams at a young age? Keep your head down. Don't color outside the lines. Fit in. Blend in. Don't live from your heart, but let your life be determined by your environment, by the judgments of others, by the way they think it should be. Make sure you can get through this life on Earth without too many bumps and bruises; then you can look back on a meaningless existence at the end of it all.

In its present form, the educational system is rapidly losing its legitimacy, in my opinion. It offers children and students prospects that are too limited. Naturally, basic skills like writing, reading, and arithmetic are extremely important. But why do you learn so little about yourself at school? About psychological insight, self-esteem, your health, communication skills, but also about earning money, meditation, and the kinds of philosophical insights that can broaden your worldview? Why do you learn so little or even nothing about your thoughts and emotions in all those years in primary and secondary school?

British professor and best-selling author Ken Robinson was known for being an international expert on creativity and innovation in education and business. His entertaining 2006 TED talk on how the educational system has been destroying talent and creativity worldwide has been watched tens of millions of times. In it, he argues that educational systems need to be overhauled because they're rooted in the outdated Industrial Age. Our current system educates us for the past and doesn't allow us to develop and make use of our personal potential. Robinson shares the story of a six- year-old girl who drew a picture of God. Her art teacher told her that no one knew what God looked like. The girl answered, "They will in a minute."

As a little girl, Dame Gillian Lynne was seen by her school as a restless and untalented child. When her mother took her to a doctor to sort out her shortcomings, he turned on the radio. Gillian started dancing spontaneously, and the doctor told the mother that her daughter was a dancer. It may well be that you've never heard of her, but not only did Gillian Lynne become a great ballerina, she's also the choreographer of my favorite musical, *The Phantom of the Opera*, and the blockbuster *Cats* as well. So many people have creativity and talents that go unused or, worse still, are suppressed and brushed under the rug.

According to the standard system of assessment, I wasn't a particularly bright student. If I'd walked the life path predicted for me on the basis of that, I would've silently faded into the background, an invisible, average achiever. Hardly any attention was paid to my high-spirited ambition and creative potential. What about you? Perhaps the educational system and you don't or didn't match. Maybe your grades don't or didn't predict a bright future. Maybe you often hear or heard that you're not good enough or that you "can't do that."

It's been demonstrated that education and knowledge are not precursors to success and wealth. Countless entrepreneurs and celebrities either didn't excel at school or left school early. Many of the most prosperous people have had little formal education. Their success is mainly the result of resourcefulness, courage, imagination, perseverance, and unshakable self-confidence.

What is the role of education? Indian spiritual teacher Jiddu Krishnamurti asked this question. Being able to think freely, without fear, without strict rules, you can discover for yourself what is really true. If you're afraid, you'll never be intelligent, he says. Intelligence is different from knowledge. Intelligence is wisdom. You can read all the books in the world, but that won't make you more intelligent. Intelligence arises when you gain insight into the processes of the mind, when you develop personal insight. This is only possible when you are spiritually free, free of fear, when you are filled with love. Only when you have a calm mind will you be able to really perceive; in those moments, your mind is sensitive to unique beauty. Perhaps that is one of the keys to our spiritual freedom.

This book is about insight, awareness, and achieving targeted results. It shows you how your behavior and mindset have programmed themselves. I call this your personal operating system. It's your conditioning, a collection of beliefs that shape your reality. You'll discover that, without your knowing it, you've been partially programmed with the wrong software and corrupted files—thought patterns that are based on inaccuracies or associations upon which you base your truth. Just like your phone and computer sometimes just freeze up, it's possible that you may feel like you "jam up" from time to time. If that's so, it's time to run a personal update.

What's important is that you discover that you can be free of the mindset imposed on you, a mindset that has unconsciously shaped your behavior and thought patterns over the years, your social-emotional conditioning. That you understand that the meaning you assign to thoughts and situations is a choice. That you gain clear insights into your own way of thinking so you can discover that you can change the way you think and the meaning you assign your thoughts. Then you'll see that you can consciously choose what you really want, without fear and limitations. It's about spiritual growth that shows you the path to success and happiness.

A Message to Humanity

I wrote this book for another reason as well. If more people begin living according to the philosophy I describe, I believe we can create a much more beautiful world to live in together. You may have noticed that a shift is happening in human consciousness. There's a growing awareness that something needs to change—in how we treat our planet, how we interact with each other, and how we care for ourselves. A growing number of people are beginning to live more consciously. More and more people are meditating, practicing yoga, and choosing healthier lifestyles. We're becoming more conscious of the need for a sustainable society.

If we don't curb our excessive consumption, we will literally consume ourselves to death in the wealthier parts of the world. It's already clear that most of the diseases in these areas are the result of unhealthy diets. The food industry, sadly, isn't focused on keeping us healthy. Its aim is for you and me to consume as much as possible, and for decades, supermarket shelves have been stocked with highly processed, unhealthy options.

What do you think happens when toxic substances are pumped into our bodies year after year, generation after generation? Maybe there's a connection between that and the staggering number of cancer cases and other serious illnesses. I'm not saying unhealthy lifestyles are the sole cause of these diseases, but common sense tells us that fresh fruits and vegetables are far better for you than processed, manufactured "food."

Fortunately, more and more healthy food options have become available to us in the past few years, but in the end, we choose what we buy and eat. Too many people still fill their bodies with unhealthy junk. The self-healing capacity of the human body and mind cannot cope with this onslaught of harmful substances. Healthier lifestyles are thus an urgent necessity. Besides that, vast amounts of food are tossed out as waste while millions of people starve to death. More even distribution of food production and consumption would lead to more harmony on our beautiful planet.

Because of unhealthy food and lifestyles, many people in our Western world are suffering, both mentally and physically. You would think that the massive pharmaceutical industry could make everyone better. Yet, as strange as it may sound, the primary goal of this industry isn't to make people healthy. Yes, they develop medications that can help, but if everyone were truly healthy, their business model would collapse. This isn't just my personal opinion. Over the years, I've spoken with many doctors and experts, and this perspective is widely shared.

Don't get me wrong—I'm not against medications. Many people benefit greatly from them, and I know individuals whose quality of life has improved because of the right treatments. But the reality is, health isn't the main priority of the pharmaceutical industry.

The word "industry" itself tells you a lot: food industry, pharmaceutical industry, oil industry, weapons industry. These industries generate billions upon billions globally. And when you look closely, you realize that most of them don't have humanity's or our planet's best interests at heart.

The arms trade, for example, keeps a large portion of the global economy running. Weapons, power, and wars have been around for as long as human history—the eternal battle between good and evil, between "us" and "them." But this conflict isn't only external. It also exists in our inner world, within our thoughts. Because the reality we experience is first created in our minds. Everything we see in the world around us begins in the individual mind and is shaped by our collective thoughts—what we call the collective consciousness.

Now imagine if we could uncover all the hidden agendas within governments, political structures, and other unseen forces behind global politics. What truths would be revealed if all those interests came to light? And, more importantly, would you be able and willing to accept that truth?

We don't need to worry about the future of Mother Earth. She survived for billions of years before human feet ever even walked upon her. And even if humanity wipes itself out, the planet will continue to exist for billions of more years. What matters in this twenty-first century is the survival of humankind. And that mission is up to us. Will we allow ourselves to be ruled by foolishness and greed, or by intelligence and wisdom?

Here's how I see it: The time in which we are now living is the time of the great clean-up, both for humankind and for Mother Earth. The establishment, made up of institutional, economic, financial, educational, political, and religious groups, is losing its credibility, power, and influence. In response to this, we now see that all the old institutions that preside over the people of this world are doing everything they can to maintain their positions of power. The games being played, and those behind them, are not entirely clear. Is it true that the world is ruled by only a few extremely powerful and wealthy individuals? Who, or what, are these invisible forces, then?

It's time for a new awakening of consciousness. Let's strive to be sensible, kind, and tolerant. Let's care for one another without feeling the need to control or interfere in every aspect of other people's lives. If we can understand and respect each other, judge less, avoid rushing to conflict, and take the time to appreciate the beauty that surrounds us, we will begin to create a more peaceful world.

Humanity needs love and wisdom now more than ever. This begins with a belief in the possibility of a better, more beautiful world. Belief controls life. Even the simple act of collectively imagining such a world can have a profound and positive impact.

We all originate from the same Divine Source of Life. We are each connected to it, yet so many of us live as though we are separate—moving through life in fear and resistance rather than in trust and loving awareness. My hope is that this book will help you to see with your heart, to remember that we—all of us, right here, right now—have the ability to create Heaven on Earth. But first, we must come to understand who we truly are and why we are here, allowing ourselves to reconnect with that infinite, loving Source that guides us all.

We—you, me, and the whole of humankind—have to understand that we can only improve the world if we all do our part. Yet you needn't worry about improving the world; just improve yourself. It will make you a happy and satisfied human being, and with this, you'll contribute to the happiness of the world.

It seems like those kinds of insights only really sink in when we are faced with our impending death. I was deeply touched by an anonymous farewell letter on the internet, which requested the message be shared with the world.

"I will soon be gone forever. That's fine, as long as someone reads this. I am 24 years old, but I have already chosen my last necktie. I will be wearing it to my funeral in a few months. The cancer diagnosis came too late. I understand that the most important thing about death is that you have to make sure you leave the world behind a bit better than before. Before, I was always too busy, but when I heard how little time I had left, I realized what really matters in life. So, I'm writing to you for a selfish reason. I want to give my life a bit of meaning by sharing what I've learned.

"Don't waste your time on work that doesn't bring you joy. It's clear that you won't be successful in something you don't like doing. Patience, passion, and dedication come when you do something you really love. It's stupid to be afraid of what other people think. Fear paralyzes and weakens you. If you let fear affect your life, it will grow until nothing but the empty shell of your life remains. Listen to your inner voice and follow your own path. Some people will think you a fool, others a hero.

"Take your life into your own hands. Take responsibility for the things that happen to you. Limit bad habits and live healthily. Let yourself be influenced by the choices you've made, not by the things you cannot control.

"Value the people around you. Your friends and family will always be an inexhaustible source of love and strength. That's why you should always cherish them.

"Leave your mark on life. Lead a meaningful life, whatever that may mean to you. The world in which we are born is a beautiful playground where everything's possible. But we are not here forever. Enjoy your time here."

The Keys to Mastering Your Mindset

- **Success requires resilience:** Achieving a successful, meaningful life involves overcoming setbacks, challenges, and personal lows, but persistence leads to rewards, including financial freedom.
- **Key ingredients for success:** Access to the right knowledge, insights, role models, and extraordinary teachers is crucial for creating a fulfilling and successful life.
- **Self-mastery through mindset:** Mastering your mindset is the foundation for success, happiness, and personal growth, as thoughts shape reality and influence behavior.
- **Questions over answers:** Thought-provoking questions are more valuable than answers, encouraging reflection on life decisions and personal mindsets to guide self-discovery.

- **Awareness is key:** Increasing self-awareness helps understand personal conditioning, break negative patterns, and gain control over thoughts, emotions, and behaviors.
- **Action leads to results:** Success requires consistent effort, discipline, and applying learned principles through daily routines to achieve long-term goals.
- **Thoughts shape emotions and actions:** Thoughts guide emotions and behaviors, influencing daily actions and long-term outcomes, highlighting the importance of positive thinking.
- **The importance of clarity:** To achieve success, having a clear vision of personal desires and goals is essential to shape life intentionally and productively.
- **Belief precedes results:** Believing in yourself and in the strategies shared is the starting point for transformation and real-life changes.

*"In order to arrive where I am now,
I had to follow the path that is behind me.
Of the many roads that have led me to this moment,
I chose one, as I will choose one future
that will take me to my destination."*

PART

I

My Story

From Business to Buddha

BEFORE I TELL you in detail about my philosophy on the art of living and mindset—the primary subjects of this book—in Parts II and III, I'll first share with you how I ended up doing what I do and how I've become who I am.

It was 2007. My media company was doing great, but I was no longer having fun. I'd had it. Not just with media and entertainment, with everything. I'd worked myself to the bone for 22 years. What began as a big dream came true for too long, it felt like. I was burned out. And if there's one thing about me, it's that if I don't like doing something, I stop doing it. That's how I'm wired.

This is a piece of advice I want to share with you early on: do what you love to do as much as you can. And if you realize you're doing something grudgingly, just stop doing it. Otherwise, it will consume massive amounts of energy and only lead to negative thoughts.

I started hanging out on my boat whenever I could, dreaming of sailing away. It had been my long-cherished dream, and it was granted. A few months later an interested enterprise offered to take over my media company. Our shareholders were rewarded well for their contribution, and the amount that landed in my bank account would allow me to live a carefree existence for the coming years. To the outside world, I was a successful businessperson who was financially free at the age of 37. But on the inside, I was feeling burned out and exhausted. I made it clear that I didn't want to see anybody anymore. My loving girlfriend told me I was depressed, and she was right. I was absolutely no fun to be around. I wanted peace and quiet and chose to cast off. I left.

I set sail on the open sea, headed to Southern Europe. The blue waters of the sea brought freedom and peace of mind. On the third morning after leaving the north coast of Portugal, I was greeted by a dolphin leaping out of the waves next to me, and for a while it happily kept me company to the rhythm of the ocean. A thought suddenly struck me for the first time in three days. I'd just spent three days in a spiritual void, thoughtlessly keeping an eye on the wind and waves. Without thinking about it, I'd busied myself with the weather and had intuitively steered my boat south. It was, as I see it, my journey to nothingness, a journey to awareness.

Aboard I found peace of mind. Finally, there was inner silence. I look back on that experience as the moment a change started to take place within me. On my voyage, I was one with the Great Nothing. I deeply enjoyed the quiet and the peace.

I read many books in my time on board, books like the *I Ching*; the *Tao Te Ching*; *Synchrodestiny*; *The Seven Spiritual Laws of Success*; *The Little Prince*; *The Alchemist*; *Initiation*; *The Seven Habits of Highly Effective People*; *Screw It, Let's Do It*; *The Science of Getting Rich*; *As a Man Thinketh*; and, for the umpteenth time, *Think and Grow Rich*.

From the Atlantic Ocean, I sailed past Gibraltar to the Mediterranean Sea. Those nautical miles brought me clear insights. I was in charge of my boat, but I couldn't change the circumstances around me—too much wind, waves that were too high, dark nights that were too long—I could only control how I handled those situations. Getting angry or being afraid did nothing to change the circumstances; either one would only alter my perception of things. I couldn't change the wind, so I'd adjust my sails or change course.

I dropped anchor in Barcelona in the autumn of 2010. I loved the city so much that I decided to stay there for the winter months to write my first novel. I had a reason for writing that book—I had a story to tell about the immortality of pure love and the transience of our existence. During the three-year writing process, a second reason arose. I wanted to prove that the strategy I'd developed would lead to success once again, this time through the book.

A close friend recommended I start a writing course at a renowned writing school in Amsterdam. I needed a teacher because I'd never written before. I started with a crystal-clear goal for myself: I wanted to reach 100,000 readers and have it in the top 10 novels on the bestseller list.

Every few weeks, I flew from Barcelona to Amsterdam to take writing classes. The teacher, Mr. B., was armed with a red pen.

First, he scrapped sentences and then completed chapters from my manuscript. Writing isn't easy. I noticed that my teacher asked a lot of questions—good questions. They developed my psychological insight and taught me to quickly see what people actually mean, which is often different from what they say.

In Barcelona I wrote for hours on end and enjoyed the sunny life on my boat. Most afternoons found me at an outdoor café on the Joan de Borbó, near the marina. I met many passersby, mostly tourists. Our talks largely centered on personal questions and problems. What surprised me about these conversations was that most of the people I was talking to—students in their twenties, go-getter thirty-somethings, and mid-lifers in their forties—had no idea how they wanted to fill the years ahead of them. They seemed to be spending their days drifting aimlessly. More and more, I discovered that very few people really had a specific dream they were living for. Or they didn't believe it was achievable. Most of them had no clear answer when I asked what their ideal life looked like. Did they not know, or were they afraid to say?

Have you ever really thought about what your ideal life would look like? Not that the rest of your life has to be mapped out, but how and where do you see yourself in a year's time, or five years from now? Do you have a dream? What does your best life consist of? How are you going to make that happen?

I sailed around the Mediterranean for three summers. I met my wife, Cindy, at that time, not knowing that meeting her would radically alter the course of my life. Cindy joined me sailing for a few weeks. We spent most of our time anchored around Mallorca and Ibiza. She immersed herself in the on-board library. She read for days on end. One evening, while we were enjoying the sunset, she asked me, "Why did I never learn this at school? Why aren't you teaching these things?" I paused for thought, but I answered that I was going to sail around the world.

Moreover, I had a book to finish first, and that book contained the lessons I wanted to share.

After three years of hard work, my novel, *Dancing in Heaven*, was finally finished. Had it not been for my teacher, Mr. B., who then became my editor, it would never have happened. The importance of a good teacher was brought home to me again. A good teacher isn't someone who joins in the conversation or showers you with compliments. Mr. B. was strict and pointed out my numerous mistakes and shortcomings. Only when you're able to see and understand what you're not doing right are you able to grow.

Still, I was preoccupied by Cindy's question: "Why aren't you teaching these things?" All those passersby I'd met in Barcelona, people who'd come to me with questions, people who'd listened to my stories: Were they all signs, or was that all one big bunch of coincidences?

What did I want? Did I still want to drift around on my boat for years? Or did I want to write and speak? What expert could I better ask than my own business mentor? I booked a $10,000 seminar with Dan Peña (in May 1999), a distinguished-looking man with gray hair, full of charisma, always dressed in a three-piece suit and tie. He was a self-made American businessperson who became a multimillionaire. I'd first met him at a crucial moment in my life when I'd lost all my money through a foolish move on the stock exchange. I was $2 million in debt, and my future seemed hopeless. Until I met him: Mr. Peña.

Fourteen years later, in September 2013, I found myself sitting across from him again in his castle in Scotland. Peña gave me three assignments: to write down what decision I was going to make that week, to determine my goals for the next five years, and to recognize the patterns in my life. He quoted Steve Jobs' words: "You can't connect the dots looking forward; you can only connect them looking backward. So, you have to trust that the dots will somehow connect in your future."

Writing leads to clarity and insight, so I put my life on paper—because there is, of course, also the story of my life before I became a well-known person in media land. Let me start at the beginning.

"First you have to be it before you can become it."

Wizard and Millionaire

I was born in Gdynia, Poland in 1969. My father's parents lived on a farm that had no running water, and electricity was rarely used because there wasn't enough money for it. They used wood to heat the house and cook.

My mother is Dutch and couldn't adjust to the dreary Communist existence. It wasn't easy, but eventually my parents moved to the Netherlands. I can't remember much about that time, but we didn't have much. I grew up with my grandmother. She showered me with love and attention and believed in me unconditionally.

When I was in grade school, I told my teacher I wanted to be a wizard and a millionaire when I grew up. The teacher thought I wasn't being serious. The feeling was mutual.

Every seven-year-old understands that you can become a wizard. But how could I have known that I also wanted to become a millionaire? When you're so young, you're unaware of money or happiness. Nevertheless, seemingly insignificant events can leave lasting impressions. They can be of great importance to you later in life.

We had a good life, just like the rest of our family and most of the people living on our street. Our life in the Netherlands was paradise. I became aware of that when we went back to the country of my birth for the first time since we had left. It was 1980, and I was 10. Eastern Europe was still behind the Iron Curtain. People were lined up in front of shops, and scarcity reigned.

We went to visit a great-aunt who lived in a gray apartment building. Her little living room contained a wooden table and four chairs. She and countless other people who all turned out to be family welcomed us warmly. This old lady and her siblings had saved food for days to share everything they had with us. The table was full of homemade bread, cake, and cookies. I couldn't understand a thing, but I could feel their happiness. Only years later did I understand the inestimable value of this way of living: if you're willing to share everything you have with joy, your heart will be filled with pure happiness. I learned that wealth isn't about how much you own, but about how much you give.

At the same time, I also discovered that money does determine your living comfort to a great extent. Money may not make people happy, but it does largely determine the course and substance of your life. My Uncle John was a businessperson. He traded in stocks, currency, and oil. He had no job and no boss, but he earned a truckload of money. Until things went wrong. He had taken risky trading positions, which had led to disastrous consequences. From one day to the next, he lost his luxury car, his money, and his friends—he didn't even have a house. He moved in with us. The only place for an extra bed was in my room, in the attic.

He worked day and night, and his standard of living quickly bounced back to its old level. Shortly after his renewed success, he died of a heart attack. Uncle John, though I didn't know him well, made an unforgettable impression on me. He became my role model. Because of him, I chose a life of wealth. Only recently did it become clear to me that I'd already become a millionaire when I was seven years old. It was the moment I had made the decision to start living "a rich life." That was incredibly decisive for my mindset, my mentality, and my vision of life. This experience wrote the program for my personal operating system in my subconscious. From then, it took 20 years to actually earn that first million.

You can only become something when you've decided in your mind that you are that thing. You have to be able to see and feel yourself the way you want to be to make that vision happen. You have to first be it before you can become it.

Radio Business

The magic of radio drew me in when I was in high school. I was 13 and had discovered my life's mission. I was spending most of my time making music and playing DJ, although my father would have preferred that I spent more time on schoolwork. He thought I should be thinking about my future and wanted me to go to college, but my grades didn't justify that desire of his.

I was fortunate. At an early age, I became a popular DJ at the number-one radio station in the Netherlands. I was living my passion with heart and soul, enjoying fleeting fame and princely sums of money.

Life felt like a blessing. I fell in love and got married at 23, in the mid-1990s. The studios of Radio 538 and The Music Factory were magnets for celebrities. I met Giorgio Armani, The Spice Girls, The Backstreet Boys, Sandra Bullock, Mariah Carey, Janet Jackson, Celine Dion, and many more. But as the station's commercial success grew, my passion for radio began to fade. By the time I was 29, I found myself wondering: Can I still be doing this work at 40? And if not, then what? It seemed like it was time to start thinking about my future.

Seeking advice, I turned to sensible businesspeople, self-made millionaires, and seasoned real estate investors. They advised me to invest in real estate. But the bank's investment advisers had a different plan: stocks, options, and an investment mortgage. Ignoring the sound advice I'd received, I poured all my savings into the stock market instead. The bank even offered to lend me more money, convincing me I could turn an even faster profit. The market was only going one way—up.

Just months later, I received a devastating message from the bank. The stock market had collapsed, and I was asked to repay several hundred thousand dollars immediately. I couldn't. The bank sold off all my shares and options, the whole kit and caboodle. That horrific loss led to a debt of almost $2 million. Not for the bank, though—for me.

> *"If you're willing to share everything you have with joy,*
> *your heart will be filled with pure happiness."*

Valuable Life Lessons

In a panic, I called my business mentor, Wim, asking for advice (or rather, for money). He reminded me of something he had already told me: *Don't mess with things you don't understand.* It was a painful life lesson. When I asked him if I could borrow money, he didn't answer. Now, years later, I understand why. One of the most valuable lessons I've ever learned: *Never lend money to someone who can't manage it.* Wim helped me by not helping me.

We did, however, take his Bentley to meet with the bank director. Years earlier, I had purchased an old farm with a house in need of serious renovation. To cover the debt, the bank granted an additional mortgage on the farm. The rise in property value was my temporary lifeline. Thanks to Wim's creative financial solution, the bank's issue was resolved, but I was still left wondering how I'd ever pay off that enormous debt.

During this difficult period, my emotional state hit rock bottom. My grandmother and father-in-law passed away within a short span, and my wife fell gravely ill. These events created an immense void, and I spiraled into destructive thoughts. But it was in this darkness—facing my wife's illness, the grief of losing my grandmother, and my own despair—that a burst of clarity hit me. I realized that life is the greatest gift ever given to me, and I owed it to myself and those I loved to make the absolute most of it. I felt an urgent, unrelenting drive—an invincible combination. I decided, at that moment, that I would do everything in my power to reclaim my life. Nothing and no one would stand in my way. I resolved to live my best life, for myself, for my wife, and for love.

The money was gone, but fortunately, I hadn't completely ignored all the sound advice I'd received. I had put aside enough emergency funds to last at least six months—a safety net for stormy waters. I used almost the entire amount to attend one of Dan Peña's private four-day seminars.

Peña taught me everything I needed to know to build a major company quickly and take it to the stock exchange or sell it. He calls his method the Quantum Leap Advantage.

It was the summer of 1999. Following Peña's method, my goal was to consolidate an industry. The strategy involved buying up several companies within the same sector, streamlining their operations to cut costs, and then adding significant value. My idea was to merge several television production companies, with the added value being the internet. We built a multimedia production house designed to create both television and online content. It was early 2000, during what would later be called the internet bubble. The internet was still in its infancy, and content was the magic word. The concept of offering on-demand programs online seemed futuristic and far-fetched.

I secured a $200,000 loan, which gave me just enough breathing room to cover groceries and the hefty monthly mortgage. It also provided start-up capital to launch Future Active Network. I met an investor, and through him, a second investor—two partners who were experienced in doing business and making money. The company grew rapidly.

But Mr. Peña warned me. He suspected the primary investor behind our venture was a shrewd entrepreneur and warned me that, despite my genuine drive, I was a total rookie when it came to business. My enthusiasm and pride set off alarm bells in him, and he was right.

The situation was a ticking time bomb. I could foresee a drama unfolding, so I left and started working on creating a new company, Pilarczyk Media Group (PMG)—the business I eventually sold five years later.

A New Mission

It was September 2013. I was at Peña's Guthrie Castle in Scotland, where he asked me to put my life's journey on paper. What was I going to do with the rest of my life?

Mr. Peña looked at me and said, "Pass on what you've learned."

And so, my new mission began. Teaching other people what I had learned through my own experience and all the lessons from my business mentors and spiritual teachers. Not just talking about success in life and business, but what I call the art of living. How to find answers to life's questions, how to deal with everyday problems, how to deal with emotions, knowing and understanding yourself, the power of thoughts, the science of success, the power of asking good questions, why you do what you do—and to encourage you to do what you really want to do: live your best life.

"The journey of the soul.
The beauty of departing is that you can always return.
First you dream of the departure, then of the journey,
and then you long to return to the place you departed from.
Enjoy the dream, enjoy the journey, enjoy the homecoming.
And discover that your happiness is always wherever you are."

PART

II

The Philosophy of Success and Happiness

Success and Happiness

AFTER A LONG quest for happiness and inner peace, I asked my teacher—my life coach and spiritual master—what the purpose of life was. He answered, "That you live your best life!" This became my life motto. Keep things simple. Enjoy life, have fun, keep growing spiritually, practice tolerance, live from a place of love, and be grateful. Live your best life.

According to Eastern philosophies, a happy life is the result of a balanced mix of your outer world (what happens around you, the material world), your physical world (your body), and your spiritual inner world (your mind). The mind bestows happiness, the body provides health, and the material world supplies comfort. When those three elements are in balance with each other, you will experience peace and harmony in yourself. In the remaining pages of this book, I explain how you can take a spiritual journey to discover the balance within you and lead a beautiful, successful, and happy life.

Because it's important to have a shared understanding of what we mean by these two words, I would like you to think about what your definitions of success and happiness are for a moment.

According to the *Oxford English Dictionary*, success is defined as "the accomplishment of an aim or purpose; the attainment of fame, wealth, or social status." But when I talk about success, I'm not just referring to professional or financial achievements. And when I speak of wealth, I don't mean solely money or material possessions. Money is a tool to help us lead comfortable lives, but our greatest treasures are things like freedom, wisdom, inner peace, strong friendships, loving relationships, and spiritual insights. These, to me, are the elements that truly make us happy.

Merriam-Webster defines happiness as "good fortune; a state of well-being and contentment; a pleasurable or satisfying experience." People often confuse good fortune with simple luck. Yet, good fortune could also be described as "being as prepared as possible for a desired situation, so that you know exactly what to do to achieve the results you want"—just like the best soccer players in the world are always ready to seize every opportunity to score, no matter how slim the chance may be. Good fortune and coincidence tend to appear in your life when you're clear about your goals and well-prepared to take action.

Everyone wants a beautiful, successful, and happy life. I gave that desire concrete meaning at a very young age. I wanted to be a DJ, a wizard, and a millionaire. Unfortunately, there weren't any teachers at my school who were willing or able to show me how to achieve those dreams, so I set out in search of business mentors and spiritual teachers on my own.

I wasn't much of a reader in my younger years. It wasn't until I turned 21 that I understood the value of picking up a book. But when I visited my father-in-law in Miami in the mid-1990s, I became mesmerized by the sheer scale of a Barnes & Noble bookstore. A whole new world opened up to me. I was immediately drawn to books on personal development and success, with titles like *How to Think Like a Millionaire, Don't Worry, Make Money, Success Is a Choice,* and *Think and Grow Rich.* That last title, written by Napoleon Hill in 1937, had the biggest impact on me. I read it three times in a row and discovered a treasure trove of wisdom. *Think and Grow Rich* significantly shaped the course of my life.

> *"You become what you believe.*
> *Not what you hope for, what you want,*
> *or what you wish for.*
> *You become what you are convinced of,*
> *deep down inside."*

The Power of Thoughts

I became a diligent student of *Think and Grow Rich.* The book focuses on the power of your thoughts and how you can harness them to turn your dreams and desires into reality. It fascinated me—the idea that thoughts are things and that through imagination, you can shape your reality. Napoleon Hill lays out 13 principles that together form a strategy for success.

He frequently wrote about "the mind." You can think of the mind as your personal cloud, an infinitely vast, virtual repository that holds all your thoughts and experiences. Imagine it as an invisible cloud of energy-filled thoughts floating around you. That cloud is charged with energy and can connect with what Hill refers to as Cosmic Consciousness, or Infinite Intelligence.

I couldn't put the book down—I felt an enormous sense of recognition. From the very first page, I realized that I had unconsciously followed those same principles to achieve my dream of working for radio. I had a burning desire, an unwavering belief in myself, and was absolutely convinced I would succeed. I could vividly see myself working in the radio studio—it felt so real I could almost taste it. Without being aware of it, I had been preparing for that opportunity for years, structuring my subconscious for success. Even though the world saw it as a mission impossible, I was determined to make it happen.

The philosophy of the power of thoughts, the law of attraction, and the manifestation of our imagination is a recurring theme in many success books. I found fascinating parallels between Hill's work and earlier writings, such as *The Master Key System* (1912) by Charles F. Haanel, *The Science of Getting Rich* (1910) by Wallace D. Wattles, *Thoughts Are Things* (1889) by Prentice Mulford, and *As a Man Thinketh* (1903) by James Allen.

In all these books, written around 1900, the central theme is that our reality and existence are a direct result of our thoughts. Everything originates from thought. Another striking similarity is how the authors speak of a Formless Source—a Higher Power—whose energy is the wellspring of the entire universe. Everything flows from this single source, an intelligent energy that underpins all creation. A full century later, this line of thinking was skillfully revived by Rhonda Byrne in *The Secret* (2006).

The combination of professional success and the spiritual deeply fascinated me. From that point on, I filled my shelves with books like *The Alchemist* by Paulo Coelho, *The Prophet* by Kahlil Gibran, *The 7 Habits of Highly Effective People* by Stephen Covey, and *The Seven Spiritual Laws of Success* by Deepak Chopra, alongside books on Buddhism and Taoism. What stands out about Chopra is his ability to connect spiritual laws with success and wealth creation.

Some of these bestselling authors have shared that they have shared that they "receive inspiration from above," which they then use to write their books. When I spoke to Deepak Chopra for our *Live Your Best Life* podcast, he told me that he literally receives texts, which he then only has to write down himself. So that's that somewhat difficult-to-explain contact with Cosmic Consciousness that many artists and performers use. Or have access to—if you want to call it that.

I was searching for the path to both success and wealth, as well as happiness and wisdom. Initially, these seemed like two separate journeys, but I soon realized they share common origins and stem from the same mindset. The path to happiness and wisdom is a spiritual one, as old as time itself. Buddha teaches us that happiness is not dependent on what we own or our status, but on how we think and manage our life energy. He also emphasizes that desire is the root of suffering; the more we long for, the more we struggle. By wanting less, living with greater awareness, and striving less, we free ourselves from this cycle. The key is to strike a balance between our physical, spiritual, and material worlds. This involves maintaining a healthy body and a clear mind, and transforming your intentions into physical action.

Napoleon Hill believed that you must be incredibly determined to reach your goals, while Buddha taught the opposite—that you must let go. These views may seem contradictory, but they share a key similarity: do what you love, follow your heart, and live from a place of passion. There's also one common denominator: the mind. Buddha teaches that we reflect our souls and minds, and that our thoughts drive our existence. Your imagination creates your reality—you become what you are convinced of, deep down, not what you hope for or want.

James Allen echoes this in *As a Man Thinketh* (1903), explaining that we don't attract what we want, but what we are. I felt like a millionaire years before I actually became one. At seven, I made the irreversible decision to become one, and from then on, it was just a matter of accumulating wealth. No athlete wins gold without already seeing himself as a champion. This isn't about wishing or desire; it's about being deeply convinced of the reality you want. Every action and feeling begins with a thought, and as Allen said, a person is literally what they think, with their personality shaped by cumulative thoughts.

Clear Thinking

I was reading *Think and Grow Rich* for the zillionth time when, suddenly, I saw it. "Think" is right there. Think. Not hoping and wishing that you'll grow rich. Not sit on your butt and grow rich. And not do something and wait and see. It's about thinking, and we've lost that capacity. We may think we think, but in fact, we mostly worry about all the worst-case scenarios we can conjure up. We visualize what can go wrong and generate inner fear. We worry about what others think of us. What we actually do is focus our attention entirely on the outside world. That has nothing to do with thinking.

Thinking is going within. It's a skill that helps you solve challenges. If you can't find an answer, you have to ask a better question. That means you have to first formulate your question as clearly and specifically as possible and write it down. Focus on your inner world. That's where you'll find most of the answers. Take time to ponder and not to think. Free up time to meditate, create space in your head. Then you will see that inspiration will come to you. Once you've grown skilled in this method, it'll bring clarity and insights. As a result, fear and uncertainty will disappear and your confidence will grow. From that positive state, you'll dare to make your own, right-for-you decisions. And every decision you make determines the direction of your life.

> *"Life is a journey, and every journey*
> *needs a destination.*
> *This destination is not a place,*
> *not an end point,*
> *but a way of life."*

Can You Design Your Own Life?

Life is a journey, and every journey needs a destination. This destination is not a place, not an end point, but a way of life. The ancient Chinese philosophers called it the Tao. Life is the Way, a path of life you walk by climbing towering mountains and overcoming deep valleys. The Way is created as it is walked. The Way has side roads and sometimes crossroads. Those are the moments you have a choice to make.

Do you have freedom of choice? Is your life predestined? Or is everything merely a coincidence? Our existence is part of an immense, systematic whole: the universe. The fact that all the stars and planets move in a certain way within an ever-expanding universe, that the sun and the moon circulate in a predictable pattern—and have done so for eons—is that all just a coincidence? Humankind has wrestled with questions about the origin of our cosmos since becoming capable of thought. Even great scientists, including Einstein and Copernicus, and wise men such as Lao Tzu and Socrates have been unable to find an answer.

Is your life predestined? Is it a show taking place without you having any influence on it? Is the course of your life described in the Great Book of Truth, the Akashic records? It's possible, but not every aspect of our lives can be predestined, because we do actually make choices ourselves.

"Of the many paths that have led me to this moment, I chose one, just as I will choose one future that will bring me to where I am going," says the *Tao Te Ching*, the most important scripture of Taoism. This book dates from the sixth century BCE. The texts were handed down orally for 300 years, and subsequently written down. Lao Tzu is considered the spiritual father of Taoism.

The texts show that our life path is created as we walk it. It is the path that is shaped by the choices you make.

In my view, there are two ways to walk this path.

You either 1. determine the goal and move in that direction, or 2. go on an adventure and see where you end up.

Think back to your personal operating system, and you'll understand that the information you put in it is particularly decisive. The course of your life is largely up to you. Of course, it depends on your personal circumstances as well. A serious accident or illness can have a major impact on your physical and mental state. Those may restrict you, but in that case, too, I'm convinced that your inner strength and mindset determine your success and happiness. I'm not saying it's easy. I'm also not saying that everything is possible for everyone, but I do know that a combination of a positive mental attitude and a zest for life can be miraculous.

People sometimes ask me how the philosophy I share applies to those living in war zones or enduring famine. In these situations, you can't simply say, "Live your best life!" because their immediate priority is survival. Human beings have universal needs, as outlined by American psychologist Abraham Maslow in his 1943 publication, *A Theory of Human Motivation*. At the most basic level, we need food and water. Next comes safety and security. Once these are met, we seek social connection, recognition, and appreciation. After that, we strive for material possessions and financial stability. Beyond this, we focus on personal development, expanding our mental capacity, with the final phase being self-realization or spiritual growth.

In our relatively comfortable lives, the quality of our existence often depends more on our reactions than on our circumstances. As the Stoic philosopher Epictetus, who lived in the first century CE, said, "It's not the circumstances, but how you react to them." While we may not always have control over what happens, we do have control over how we respond. Often, within challenges lie hidden opportunities.

We all face frustrating and unpleasant moments in daily life, and I liken this to the weather and nature. Life, like the seasons, follows a pattern. For as long as we can remember, summer gives way to autumn, which is followed by winter. Winters can be mild or harsh; summers can be scorching or humid. There may be long stretches of cloudy days, but the sun always returns. No matter how hopeless a situation might feel, there's usually a light at the end of the tunnel. But it's also true that in most cases, you need to take action—either to change the situation or to change your perception of it. Learn to withstand autumn's storms, survive winter's chill, prepare for the rebirth of spring, and savor the joys of summer. Embrace the cycles of life. They come and they go.

"It's not about what you do, but how you do it."

Doing Something in a Certain Way

You can do all kinds of things, and you can even do them well, but to achieve true success, it's not just about what you do—it's about doing it in a certain way. Bob Proctor often said, "It's not what you do, it's the way you do it." The way you approach something determines whether you succeed or fail, which is exactly what Wallace D. Wattles writes about in *The Science of Getting Rich*. Success is not in the action itself, but in how the action is carried out.

Cindy and I recently experienced something that perfectly illustrates this. We were dining at our favorite restaurant. Normally, we're served by a specific waiter who always elevates the experience. But that evening, he wasn't there. Instead, a polite young woman served us. She did everything right according to the book. She was courteous, friendly, and professional—but there was a noticeable distance. Perhaps she was new or lacked confidence, but everything she said felt rehearsed. She described each dish precisely, yet it sounded like she was reciting lines she had memorized, rather than speaking from her own understanding. It felt robotic, devoid of passion. Although she followed every step perfectly, her presentation didn't connect with us.

The next time we visited, the other waiter was there again. He served us with passion and confidence, telling us about each dish with enthusiasm and a personal touch. His stories engaged us, and he created a sense of connection. Do you see the difference? Both waiters performed their job well, following the rules flawlessly. Yet, there was a vast difference between the two experiences—between good and extraordinary. The difference is in doing something "a certain way."

That's the key to moving from good to great, from average to exceptional. It's not just about doing the job right; it's about doing it with mastery, intention, and presence. That's what you must learn to feel, develop, and refine to join the ranks of the very best at what you do.

Take coffee shops, for example. There are countless independent cafés that serve better coffee than Starbucks. Yet Starbucks has achieved worldwide success not because it has the best coffee, but because of *the way* it does business—its ability to create a consistent experience across the globe, foster a sense of community, and build a recognizable brand. It's the atmosphere, the reliability, and the way it makes customers feel that keeps people coming back. That's the power of doing things in a certain way.

We had a painter working on our house, but he approached it like he was Picasso—pouring passion and dedication into every stroke. That's the key difference between someone who's simply doing a job and someone who takes pride in their craft.

Whatever you do, do it with passion and dedication. That will make you stand out from the crowd.

There are many people who sing, play sports, make music, act, and write. Yet not everyone achieves the results that Beyoncé, Drake, Cristiano Ronaldo, Tom Brady, J.K. Rowling, and Dan Brown have. Further research has shown that these well-known people have something in common. They do something in a certain way.

Following Napoleon Hill's lead, I began to study numerous successful people and businesses. I started this back when I was working in radio and television. I met many celebrities, and I discovered similarities and patterns in "their" ways of being. The patterns that can be seen when you juxtapose the life histories of many successful people boil down to the principles in *Think and Grow Rich.*

It shows that success is largely the result of applying a number of practical principles in the areas of the power of thought, belief and conviction, desire, imagination and auto-suggestion, specialized knowledge, structured planning, decisiveness, persistence, and the use of your subconscious and your sixth sense. Applying these principles leads to a certain way of thinking, which then determines how you act.

When I was living in Barcelona, there was this little square near the marina. Every morning, I would go there to get a sandwich and an apricot pastry from Baluard bakery. There was a line stretched out to the sidewalk every day, and on Saturday mornings, you could easily find yourself waiting in it for over a half an hour. There were two other bakeries on that same little square. They never had lines. Three bakeries within a hundred yards of each other. What made Baluard so distinctly different?

It smelled amazing, it looked really nice, you saw the bakers working on their craft with pleasure and love, and the ladies behind the counter were particularly warm and welcoming. And apart from all that, you felt this invisible, magnetic attraction. They weren't just baking any old bread and pastries; they were doing something in a certain way.

Coincidental Luck or Doing It a Certain Way

Over the years, I've spent more time studying the lives of successful people, and it became clear to me that they all did things in a certain way. There were distinct patterns. Many of them faced tough beginnings—financial struggles, a lack of formal education, difficult life experiences, or repeated rejections and setbacks. Yet they didn't let these obstacles define them or hold them back.

Were these individuals simply lucky? Was I lucky? Certainly. No one achieves success without a bit of luck. But is success solely down to good fortune? I've asked close friends who live prosperous lives if they consider themselves lucky, and without fail, they all say yes. My friend Wim, who supported me during my own financial crisis, believes luck played a role in his success. He left school early, became a truck driver, and eventually found his way into waste management. He later started his own company, which he sold for tens of millions. But it wasn't just luck that got him there. Wim faced countless setbacks, worked incredibly hard, and is an expert in practical, straightforward thinking.

Someone else I know who hadn't spent much of his youth in school either told me that he'd by chance met someone who'd taught him about commerce. This was in the early 1990s, just as cell phones were hitting the market. He started trading and selling these new tech devices. As a result, he was able to earn a great deal of money, which formed the basis of his very comfortable current existence. According to him, that one encounter was crucial to the course of his future life. Is that simply luck?

The most delightful story comes from a close friend of mine who built an incredible textile company. Rob looks back with great contentment on having lived a fulfilling life. However, at 17, he had no idea what he wanted to do. One day, when he was hitchhiking, a car stopped, and Rob got in. As he talked with the driver, a man he'd never met before, the man offered him a simple job as a gofer, a jack-of-all-trades. Rob accepted the offer, carefully observed what was going on around him, learned, gained experience, and started his own business a few years later. His work became his passion, and as a result, he created a very successful and happy life for himself.

Reflecting on this, I realize I was fortunate as well. My greatest luck was discovering my passion for radio early on. That passion gave my life direction. Over time, I discovered that my passion for radio didn't have to last a lifetime. It didn't disappear, but it did fade. A new passion didn't reveal itself right away, but the need to earn a living was there. At that point, I drifted into a void, questioning what I wanted to do with the rest of my life. Slowly, a new passion emerged—the desire to write, speak, and guide others toward living their best lives.

So, in my opinion, true success comes when you align your thoughts, beliefs, and actions with the outcome you desire. It's not just about what you do, but how you do it—approaching everything with a mindset of abundance, confidence, and belief that you're already achieving your goals.

> *"Your mind is like fertile earth upon which*
> *you would like colorful flowers to bloom,*
> *but on which problems and negative thoughts*
> *spread like weeds."*

What Do You Focus On?

What truly matters to you? I ask this question in every master class. The most common answers are health, love, appreciation, money, happiness, time, and freedom.

During economic downturns, I've seen many people suffer due to a lack of money. When that happens, their happiness vanishes. When your mind is clouded with worry and negative thoughts, there's no space for inner peace. Now, I know money isn't the key to happiness, but financial freedom opens doors to opportunities that can enrich your life in meaningful ways.

Ultimately, we all seek the same fundamental things: happiness, good health, and enough money. It's human nature to long for love and joy. We are loving beings by nature. But love is no easy feat—it can't be taught through books or courses. Love defies intellectual understanding; it can only be felt. The love most of us experience is usually confined to an emotional bond with someone, to physical affection, or perhaps divine love. True love, though, is a journey of the soul. By true love, I mean a love for the beauty of nature, for all living things, for humanity, and for the awe-inspiring mystery of life itself.

I've noticed that many people don't often allow themselves to be moved by the simple things that can leave a lasting impression. I can intensely enjoy myself just gazing at nature, at the sea, at the sun glimmering on the water. I can enjoy the splendor of flowers for minutes at a time; I can enjoy watching swans swimming in a pond. I can feel infinitely happy when my dog snuggles up against me and we do absolutely nothing but be. Enjoy passionately, feel everything very deeply. From a place of love.

When was the last time you were captivated by the grandeur of a starry sky and a silvery moon? When were you last able to actually enjoy something quite small? When did you enjoy peace and quiet? What music last touched your heart? What last brought tears to your eyes? When did you last feel a tingling sensation of happiness pulsing through your body?

Yet, surprisingly, people often focus on the negative. They're quick to notice what others say, what others think, or how they react—or don't react. It doesn't take much to wound someone or upset them. A lack of love, low self-confidence, or a bit of criticism can open the floodgates, allowing negativity to seep into the mind.

Your mind is like fertile earth upon which you would like colorful flowers to bloom, but on which problems and negative thoughts spread like weeds. When they're given enough space, they'll take over your beautiful flower garden. Weeds are always growing in our thought gardens: negative imaginings, unwanted external influences, people who make you uneasy. Be vigilant and find a way to immediately get rid of those weeds. This book shows you how.

If you foster negative thoughts and feelings, they become dominant. What you pay attention to grows. It's difficult to divert your attention away from negative thoughts that keep showing up, so you need to be aware of those "weeds." Focus your attention on the positive, on what you do want, on solutions rather than problems, on pleasure and not (mental) pain. On love and not fear. That sounds fairly simple. But, why is it so complicated, then?

Conflicting Thoughts

My first master class, in early 2014, was mainly focused on business success and entrepreneurship. "Success Is Mindset" was the name of the seminar. Unfortunately, the first response wasn't exactly overwhelming. There were only 6 participants in those first meetings, but that gradually grew to 15, then 60, then 200, and now as many as over 3,000 people. I'm telling you this to make it clear that everyone starts small, including me. Each and every time. Growth takes time and doesn't just happen automatically.

You will have to pay loads of attention to what you do and how you do it. Make sure you add unique value to someone else's life. That is what people will spread the word about. In the beginning, you'll need patience, but eventually, many drops also fill the bucket.

Those first groups in 2014 ranged from the freshly self-employed to successful businesspeople who were running companies or had sold them. During Q&A sessions, I quickly discovered that business itself was hardly ever the issue for the participants. Many people, including successful entrepreneurs, were struggling with limitations in their inner world: conflicting thoughts, emotions, and personal values.

Marc, a lawyer, was running a successful practice and had clear plans for the future: a house on the Côte d'Azur, cruising around in a convertible, and living like a god in France. He was an intelligent and capable man, yet something was standing in his way. His energy level was low, and as a result, he didn't have the strength to make his dream come true. A low energy level leads to emotional fluctuations and inner conflicts in many people. Marc discovered that he was hampered both by his negative mindset and by being overweight. A year later, he sent me a message that he'd lost 66 pounds. He was now living consciously and healthy and feeling energetic and strong. As a result, he was sharper in business and once more achieved great success. He was in charge of his health and thoughts, and he was happy again.

Leah, a successful businessperson, arrived in a brand-new Porsche Cayenne Turbo. She told me that the money was pouring in. She also regularly took trips to luxurious destinations. Unfortunately, the photos she posted on Instagram led to jealousy among her friends. For that reason, she'd bought a more modest second car, had stopped sharing her life on social media, and was doing her best to conceal her enjoyment of life in her conversations with friends. To preserve the peace, she no longer dared to be who she actually was. Leah was 44, was stylish, and wore stunning jewelry. She was a strong woman with class and great persuasive powers, yet as she told her story, the mascara was streaming down her cheeks.

I asked her why she felt so unhappy. She explained that women with whom she'd been friends for years thought Leah's life of luxury was excessive, and she was wrestling with this. She felt a chasm growing in her close friendships. I asked how much time those girlfriends spent on their work and what goals they had. Most of them were focused on their children and family lives. That had always been their goal: to get married, have children, and lead secure, worry-free lives. There's nothing wrong with that, but Leah had other dreams. She wanted to see a lot of the world, loved luxury, and had resolved to earn a lot of money. For 20 years, she'd worked incredibly hard to make that dream come true. Now, she was able to enjoy it.

Know Who You Surround Yourself With

"Show me your friends, and I'll tell you your future." This statement highlights how the people you choose to be around shape your life. Your company can either lift you up or pull you down, depending on their mindset, values, and habits. If you're surrounded by people who inspire, challenge, and support you, you're more likely to thrive. But if your circle is filled with negativity and doubt, it becomes much harder to rise above.

Your environment is crucial—not just for material success, but for personal growth and fulfillment. So, look closely at the people around you. Do they push you toward being your best self, or drain your energy and keep you stuck? In the end, the people you surround yourself with reflect your future.

We often hold on to things, including friendships, that no longer serve us. Some friendships last a lifetime, but others, even if once meaningful, may come to an end. I believe we are passersby in each other's lives, intersecting for a time before moving on. It can be difficult to part ways, but sometimes, stepping back reveals that the first signs of distance appeared long ago, and those cracks can widen into an unbridgeable gap.

Our behavior is influenced by the people we spend time with. We tend to adapt to their energy, habits, and mindset. In many cases, you become the average of the people around you. But if you're evolving in a new direction, you'll notice it in your mindset and the results that follow, especially when personal growth no longer aligns with those in your circle.

So, who do you spend most of your time with? Who influences your decisions, reactions, and thoughts? The impact of your surroundings is often greater than you realize. Who in your life truly supports your goals? Who positively or negatively affects your progress? Take a close look at the people you surround yourself with and examine how they shape your behavior and mindset.

"Show me your friends and I'll tell you your future."

Money and Happiness

"What do you really want?" I asked Frank in a master class. I figured he was in his late thirties.

"I just want to be happy," he answered. "I don't think money is important. As long as I'm happy and can do what I want."

Frank's answer said a lot about him. Besides that, he didn't come across as energetic. He stood there limply, wearing a somber expression, and he sounded defensive.

"And what do you want to do then?" I inquired further. It's a crucial question. It's not uncommon for people to say they "just want to be happy." But what exactly does that mean?

When you say that you "just want to be happy," it means that your current situation isn't measuring up. In other words, at the moment you aren't "just happy," whereas I believe that happiness is not an ordinary thing, but an extraordinary thing. And when someone tells me that money isn't important to them, it usually means this person either has money problems or harbors negative associations toward money. For Frank, it was both. In complete contrast to his own perception, money really did matter.

From the many coaching conversations I've had, it's become clear to me that a great deal of suffering in people's lives arises from a lack of money. From an early age, there was a shortage of money in Frank's life. This pattern continued into his adult life in the form of debt. The perpetual shortfall of money hurt, and to conceal that pain, Frank had taught himself that money wasn't important to him. He'd subconsciously conditioned himself; it'd become his way of thinking. He thought this would keep the pain at bay. What actually happened was that by keeping money at a distance, he created money problems. When I pointed this out, Frank fell silent and said, "I've never looked at it like that before."

In our Western society, we devote a relatively large amount of time and attention to the material side of our existence. Money either contributes to our comfort or is a source of worries. Money has a major impact on our daily lives, especially when there's a (chronic) shortfall of it. "Money doesn't make you happy," is something you hear quite often from people who can't speak from experience. Friends and former business partners who have weathered severe financial and business storms believe that money in itself does not make us happy, but that a lack of money is guaranteed to lead to worry. My life is more enjoyable now than when I was deeply in debt, which is not to say that money by definition makes you happy. I know millionaires who are intensely happy, and I know millionaires who are completely miserable. It's about the meaning we assign to money, about the fulfillment we associate with that material wealth—that has a tremendous influence on our well-being.

"After a long search for happiness and inner peace, I asked my teacher what the purpose of life was. He answered, 'That you live your best life!'"

Don't fall into the trap of thinking that money isn't important. I understand why this misconception exists—your environment likely led you to believe it. A lack of money means that you can't do what you'd really like to do, sometimes it even means that you don't have enough money to do what needs doing. That leads to money troubles, and with those, every opportunity for inner peace disappears.

But let's be honest: What do you really know about money? What have you learned about it? And if you believe it's not important, what do you truly mean by that?

Our modern lives are mainly determined by money and time. And the way you occupy your time usually has to do with money. How much money you have or how much you need determines how much you have to work and what you can spend. Money can either lead to rest, when you're financially free, or to restlessness, when you're short on funds. How much more peace and joy would a bit more money bring you?

The Power of Silence

Man is either made or destroyed by himself. It is the choice and true application of thinking that determines whether he destroys himself with his thoughts or chooses joy, peace, and strength. The question is: What do you choose? What do you really want? Why do you do what you do? What does your best life look like? And what's stopping you?

These are not easy questions. Try to find out what you really want. You're probably not used to thinking like that. And if you're already trying, you'll soon come up against practical objections, or self-limiting thoughts or feelings. Each person has a dark and a light side. The devil in us is judgmental, indifferent, and sometimes destructive. The little angel in us is friendly, peaceful, and full of compassion. Every day is a balancing act between these two extremes.

Limiting thoughts—especially fear—and negative thought patterns can pursue us like tormentors. Because we allow these demons into our minds, they govern us. Oftentimes, you aren't even aware of how they creep in and infect your pure thinking. Negative thoughts lead to negative emotions, which then manifest themselves as fear and insecurity. Fear paralyzes and creates a sense of powerlessness. Fear is life-threatening.

Become aware of your dragons and demons, and you will be able to calm the inner whirlwind of negative thoughts. Only then can you observe your thinking purely.

Your mind dominates your thought process. It's like a river, almost always in motion. The surface is usually unsettled. Sometimes, even when appearing as smooth as glass, turbulent undercurrents may be present. Only very rarely is there total peace and quiet. By understanding that process better, you'll be better able to structure the continuous flow of your thoughts. In my lectures, I often tell the following story to illustrate this.

One day, two passersby stopped to talk to a nun who was fetching a bucket of water from a spring. They asked her what use a life of silence and seclusion was. The nun answered, "Look into this spring and tell me what you see."

The pair looked at the surface of the water and asked, "What should we see?"

After a few minutes, the nun repeated her question. "Look again into the spring and tell me what you see." The travelers looked again and said excitedly, "We see a reflection of ourselves."

"That is the power of silence," explained the nun. "The bucket upset the water. Now that the calm has returned again, you can see yourselves. The silence of meditation allows you to see yourself."

The two considered the words of the nun, who spoke again after a few moments. "Now look again into the spring."

The duo peered into the depths and called out: "We see the stones at the bottom!"

The nun smiled and nodded. "If you wait long enough and become one with silence, you can see the essence of everything. Your mind is like water. In times of unrest, it is difficult to see past the surface, but in complete peace and quiet, everything becomes clear."

Foggy Mind

Imagine a foggy morning. You're driving on the highway and can't even see a hundred feet in front of you. What do you do? Do you move into the left lane and speed up? Or do you drive at a snail's pace and keep your distance from the other vehicles? What happens to you when you can no longer see where you are and where you're going? When you no longer have a clear view on the situation?

In 2009, I decided to step away from work and spend a few years living on and sailing my boat. This decision marked a radical shift in my life. I said goodbye to my company, to my daily responsibilities and the accompanying stress, but also to the people I loved. This journey was both a deep desire and an essential step forward. A feeling I couldn't quite define told me it was time to let go. I had financial freedom and endless time, but my mind wasn't yet free—something I didn't fully realize at the time.

I planned for the journey to take me to sun-drenched spots along the Mediterranean Sea. Beyond that, it was an open adventure, where I let the wind decide each destination. I especially loved sailing on beautiful days, the sound of the water and wind, the endless horizon, and the peace and quiet. Each time I moored in a safe harbor after battling high waves and strong winds, I felt a profound sense of gratitude for having reached my destination.

One early morning, after sailing for three days and nights around the Bay of Biscay off Spain's northern coast, I found myself surrounded by a dense fog. I couldn't see past my own bow. The radar showed large cargo ships and fishing boats nearby, which made me uneasy but also more vigilant. After 12 hours, the visibility hadn't improved much, but I felt more at ease. I had adjusted to the situation, and my fear slowly gave way to confidence. I'd pushed beyond my comfort zone. The real relief came when the fog finally lifted and I could once again see the world around me. Only then did I realize where I was—and where I was going.

Imagine that much of your life unfolds in the midst of a fog bank. Due to the illusions of modern society and the ways our perceptions shape our thoughts, we often navigate through this fog without even realizing it. The constant bombardment of stimuli and the endless stream of our own thoughts create a veil of illusions that we mistakenly accept as reality. This can lead to mental confusion, fear, doubt, and uncertainty. It's usually accompanied by low energy levels, and this downward spiral leads in only one direction: down.

Unfortunately, hundreds of thousands of people in our society experience this on a daily basis. According to official statistics, millions struggle with extreme stress and burnout, while just as many rely on medications to cope with depression, anxiety, and insomnia. In such a state, clear thinking becomes impossible. And without clarity and insight, the road to success and happiness cannot be found.

> *"Watch your thoughts,*
> *they become your words.*
> *Watch your words,*
> *they become your actions.*

Watch your actions,
they become your habits.
Watch your habits,
they become your character.
Watch your character,
it becomes your destiny."

– From the tales of Lao Tzu

Mindfulness and Meditation

Meditation? Breathing? Yoga? I thought those were things for new-agers and spiritual seekers who couldn't handle the reality of everyday life. Not for me. I had no need for that stuff. But after I'd found inner peace on my sailing trips, I wanted to know more about them. I asked a holistic therapist if he could teach me to meditate. When he told me it was about looking for the boundless emptiness within, letting go of everything, and listening to my inner silence, I realized I'd done it unconsciously at sea—for weeks on end. Later I did it deliberately to reach a deeper state of consciousness.

Meditation brings your mind to rest and energizes you. It's a wonderful feeling. A peaceful one of freedom and joy. That inner peace can help you see that your life isn't some disorganized whole but a systematic continuum of moments. You become aware of the fact that every action and every choice you make in this moment has an influence on everything to come. So being as aware as possible in the here and now is of tremendous importance. By "in the here and now," I mean with your attention.

Planning for tomorrow and the future can only be done in the now. And your future changes with every decision and action you take now. Being in the now with your attention doesn't mean drifting off into the past or the future, losing yourself in fictitious, worrisome imaginings of guilt, regret, anxiety, and endless fretting about what could happen in the future. Be here now.

This book is about your mind, your thinking mind, but also about awareness. You are being aware of who you are and what you think. What thoughts zoom around in your head? Where do they come from? Why are they there, and what should you do with them? And how can you quiet that jumble of unceasing thoughts and hush those little voices in your head? There are two ways:

1. Mindfulness training
2. Asking good questions

And there's a natural sequence to that. Asking good questions is a skill that, in my opinion, you easily learn to master when you're mindful. So, let's look at that first.

Mindfulness is a state of being. I see it as a way of life. It means that your attention is in the present moment. You are fully aware of the moment; you feel your presence in the here and now. For a short while, your thoughts stop shifting restlessly in all directions, there are no judgments, and any voices in your head are silent.

Stillness in your mind, tranquility in yourself. I know from the thousands of people I've worked with that this can sound like a utopia. But just like amassing wealth, learning a language, and achieving success, mindfulness is a matter of patience and daily practice. It may take some effort at first, but over time you'll be able to reach a peaceful state of mind more quickly. Recall the nun with her bucket at the spring. When the stillness returns to the water, clarity emerges, and you can fathom your deepest thoughts.

You can practice this by taking a few moments for yourself each day. Ten minutes or so each time is enough. I recommend at least doing this at the beginning of the day and again in the evening before you go to sleep. I've recorded many guided meditations that you can use for this purpose, which you can find in our Meditation Moments app.

It might be a bit uncomfortable when you're first starting out, and you may actually feel restless in the beginning. But if you do it 10 days in a row, you'll feel calmer within. A wonderful feeling of stillness, freedom, love, gratitude, and presence will come over you. I'd never felt peace in that way until I started meditating. Now, I love to sit still for a few minutes, gaze out in front of me, and not have to do anything. I know very few people who've tried it and weren't enthusiastic about it afterward. People who had their doubts beforehand often change their minds after they've tried the meditations.

During my live events I do meditations, share breathing techniques, and take people through visualizations, things that pragmatic businesspeople and down-to-earth folks are sometimes skeptical about at first. Afterward, people come up to me to share the most wonderful experiences. Many of them experience extraordinary breakthroughs in the visualization sessions. Cindy and I have witnessed thousands of attendees undergo transformations. Anxiety and anger make way for trust, understanding, and love. Personal questions get answered. Choices become clear. Uncertainty turns into self-confidence, and chaotic thought patterns become lucid.

Clear Your Mind

Do you ever feel like your mind is overflowing—too much noise, swirling thoughts, being pulled in too many directions? Does it feel like, too often, your head is at full capacity? How often do you spend time tidying up the inside of your head, your mind? Do you have any idea what happens if you don't clear your mind on a regular basis?

I recently got a notification that my computer's memory was full. I could no longer store documents, videos, or audio files. No room to add anything new. My MacBook, without my being aware of it, had been getting slower and slower. That's what happens when you store everything in the available memory and have numerous programs (thoughts) running in the background. Without noticing it, your capacity decreases until things crash and you have to reboot.

This also happens in your mind when you don't tidy up and clean everything regularly. Just as you brush your teeth every day, you need to take some time every day to clean up your mind.

Thoughts come and go, like peaceful clouds in a clear sky or like devastating storms. Thousands of thoughts race through your mind every day, only a few of which you're aware of. These are the thoughts to which you cling. And the meaning you assign to those thoughts regulates your emotions.

You worry about what's to come. You feel terrible about that conversation you had yesterday. You feel guilty about what you did or didn't do. You're disappointed because someone or something didn't live up to your expectations. You keep suffering mental anguish from an event in your past. The uncertainty of tomorrow takes all the fun out of today. Your mind travels through time, to the past and into the future, and that makes you restless.

According to scientists, tens of thousands of thoughts pass through you every day. Fortunately, you're not aware of most of them, because the relatively small number you do perceive can trigger more than enough turmoil.

Sometimes, you can be very deeply absorbed in thought, like when you're on a long car drive in which you've suddenly noticed you're already miles further without realizing you'd driven that stretch. You weren't consciously paying attention behind the wheel, but "something" got you there. You go on autopilot like this in daily life more often than you might think. You do one thing while your mind is somewhere else.

The reverse can also be the case. You can be so in the moment on a walk in the woods that you deeply enjoy every step, the sunbeams shining through the leaves of the trees, the birds singing, the smells of nature. You're aware of every little detail in your environment. Your presence is so completely in the now that you don't even realize that you've been walking for hours.

You'll never be fully mindful 24 hours a day. But mastering your mind and your mindset do require that your thoughts and emotions don't get the best of you every time.

Mindfulness is a form of awareness training that has been practiced in Asia for thousands of years. In the 1970s, American professor Jon Kabat-Zinn introduced it to the West as mindfulness-based stress reduction (MBSR), designed for patients with chronic illnesses, pain, or fatigue who can't find relief through traditional medicine. It transformed many lives, including mine. Science has shown that the brain is plastic and changes with repeated practice. Everything you focus on grows. My Buddhist teachers emphasized that anything done or thought about often becomes practice. Stress, excuses, or anxiety can become automatic, just as practicing mindfulness can improve well-being.

What do you think happens when you recite positive affirmations daily, or when you consistently visualize your best life and practice gratitude? Everything you focus on regularly becomes ingrained in your mind—your default setting. Through daily mindfulness training, meditation, and breathing exercises, you become more aware of your surroundings and your own thoughts. Stress and anxiety diminish, and your reactions become less impulsive. With practice, emotions no longer control your behavior to the same extent, allowing you to navigate life with more clarity and calm.

Research over the last two decades has shown that meditation enhances brain power and flexibility. The prefrontal cortex, which governs analytical thinking, creativity, and problem-solving, becomes stronger, while the amygdala, responsible for stress and fear, becomes less active. This leads to greater emotional resilience. Initially met with skepticism by the medical field, mindfulness practices are now widely accepted, proving to reduce stress, anxiety, burnout, and restlessness. The benefits extend to improved sleep, positivity, focus, energy levels, and overall mental well-being.

In Silence, You Hear Everything

Everything moves at lightning speed nowadays; we live in unsettled times. That's how we experience it at least, and so that is how it is. Our perception determines our reality. Our brains have a lot to process, and the voices in our heads want to interfere with everything. There's little or no time left to let the jumble of thoughts calm down, and as a result, you start feeling even more restless. It's for precisely this reason that it's good to hit the pause button a few times a day.

We have to rest now and then—and I'm not talking about a short break in which you immediately burden your mind with personal problems or gossip. By rest, I mean a physical and mental break of a few minutes.

Take a walk in nature or find a quiet place to rest—it always helps. Step away for a moment and just be still. Even a few minutes of meditation every day, focused on breathing, can renew your energy and bring clarity. Life is about balancing intense work with deep rest, much like how music is formed by the balance between notes and silence. Close your eyes during the day, connect with your inner quiet, and in those moments, you'll find what truly makes you happy.

Meditation, mindfulness, or practicing silence isn't an instant fix like taking a pill for pain. While it does lower stress, heart rate, and blood pressure quickly, its true power lies in consistent practice. Just like sports strengthen your muscles, meditation strengthens your mind. In the beginning, distracting thoughts may flood in, much like you can't run a marathon on your first day. Over time, however, with repetition and focus, you'll experience more calmness, creativity, better sleep, and improved emotional balance, as your mind becomes more resilient and stable.

By seeking inner silence through meditation and conscious breathing, you prevent chaotic and worrisome thoughts from taking control. As I've mentioned, inner peace has become an essential part of my life. I don't live like a monk, but I've discovered that a quiet mind gives access to what I call "the temple of wisdom." Meditation connects you to your higher consciousness and Cosmic Intelligence. This state of serenity allows me to tap into a creative, mysterious source. Many inventors, musicians, and artists make use of that creative source. Albert Einstein stated that his greatest discoveries in physics were the result of inspirations that he believed came from "The Source."

Creative people often follow their feelings. But when you follow your feelings, what exactly are you following? Your intuition? And what is that then? Where does an idea come from, or a thought about something that didn't previously exist or hadn't been thought of before?

Cosmic Intelligence, as I understand it, is like a vast repository of all knowledge—the answers to every question are stored in the universe, much like data on the internet. Imagine you are a computer, and your capabilities are limited by your internal hardware. But when you connect to this "universal internet," you gain access to all the answers. The key is not to actively search for these answers but to formulate your question clearly, find silence, and let the answers come to you. In silence, you hear everything.

I know this may sound abstract or even mystical, but it's not. I'm not some kind of mystical guru; I'm a practical businessman. While I believe in being guided by a higher power, I'm also results-oriented, rational, and grounded in the practical world.

Inner peace is also a very welcome thing when making decisions. It creates space for insights so you can make the right choices. You can only make good choices consciously and from a positive state of being. If you're not in that space, your energy will be disturbed. There'll be static on the line. Odds are you'll make the wrong decision from that state of mind. Think back again to that story of the nun at the spring. Only once our cloudy thoughts are purified can we think clearly. And when we're in harmony with ourselves, we can feel clearly. That is, you're attuned to your inner needs and no longer feel any emotional or mental resistance within you, which then allows your energy to flow freely. Those are the moments when you feel comfortable in your own skin.

After I started getting into consciousness and meditation more, I met the well-known meditation teacher Davidji. He was the lead educator at the Chopra Center for Wellbeing and is author of the book *Secrets of Meditation*. He explained the principle of meditation like this: your cell phone rings, beeps, and vibrates all day long. Texts, apps, and emails stream in; you get notifications from social media. Your eyes frequently gravitate toward that little screen. What happens if you switch off the sound and vibration? All those messages keep coming in, but you don't hear or see them anymore. Meditation allows you to switch on your own silent mode now and then. Of course, it does require training and discipline to not sneak a peek anyway.

You don't always have to respond to what happens in the world around you. You don't always have to be talking. Start observing how many people constantly pump out sound without really saying anything. Most people can hardly be silent for even a few minutes. It's beneficial to learn how to do so. Discover how wonderful it is to experience the silence within you. Don't obsessively search for it; the silence will find you when you create space for it. The more space you offer, the deeper and greater the silence you experience will be.

The Power of Breathing

Breathing is the first and last thing you do in this life. Your first breath awakens you to life, and when you've exhaled your last breath, your soul and mind leave your earthly body. Life flows through you through your breathing. Perhaps it would be worthwhile to now and then be more aware of this magical, divine power that sustains your life.

Moreover, breathing gives you access to your mind. Our minds aren't tangible like our bodies. The mind is the invisible part of each of us and is many times greater than the physical body. We cannot consciously control that mind, the spirit in us, like we can our breathing. But we can calm our minds through our breathing.

I discovered this a number of years ago during a breathwork course with spiritual teacher Rajshree Patel, a teacher at The Art of Living organization. By focusing my attention very consciously on my breathing and applying a number of specific techniques, I was able to completely bring my body and mind to rest. Even people who are normally incredibly busy in their daily lives and feel chaotic in their heads suddenly feel relaxed and free of distracting thoughts after breathing this way.

To create that peace and quiet within, it's particularly important to breathe in and out, relaxedly, calmly, and deeply. Each time you breathe in, you take in fresh oxygen, which energizes you. Every time you breathe out, you exhale toxic waste from your body, so make sure you exhale completely. By focusing your attention on your breathing for a few minutes, you'll feel confusing thoughts disappear on their own accord, and you'll feel increasingly calmer within.

Your breathing is always in the now, so by consciously feeling your breathing, your consciousness is automatically brought to that "now" moment. By breathing consciously, you regain peace in your mind and body.

> *"The man who asks a question*
> *is a fool for a moment;*
> *the man who does not ask*
> *is a fool for life."*
>
> **— Confucius**

The Power of Asking Good Questions

Clarity comes when you quiet your mind, and that clarity brings insight. This insight alleviates fear and uncertainty, and trust emerges. This allows you to make conscious choices. It's about gaining insight into your way of thinking. Are you aware of the meaning you assign to your thoughts, to situations, or to events? That meaning determines how you feel, how you react, and how you act.

You might recognize this familiar refrain: "What will others think?" Once you allow that thought in, you start entertaining all sorts of scenarios. But what you imagine others would think of you is actually what you think yourself. People are generally much less concerned with you than you think.

Your mind can get quite carried away when the storyteller within gets going and conjures up every possible scenario. It's hard to be aware of everything that goes on in your own head because all kinds of thoughts constantly flash through it. They can be quite unsettling. But if you stop to contemplate any particular thought, you'll find that greater peace automatically follows. To understand yourself properly, to understand what you really think and mean, you have to simplify things. You have to dissect your thoughts and emotions until you get to the heart of the matter. You do this by asking good questions. If you know what you have to ask, you will also know the answer.

Unclear questions always lead to unclear answers. Our problem is that we don't know how to ask good questions and that we don't think about the questions, only about the answers. A good question is a way to solve a problem. That's because a problem is nothing more than a question to which you don't yet have a good answer. If you know how to ask the right question, you'll be able to understand. If you don't know how to formulate a good question, you can come up with an answer, but that doesn't mean you'll understand its essence. In other words, don't look for answers, but ask the right questions.

Here's an example to illustrate what I mean. Suppose that you sense that you're afraid of something. Then ask the following questions: "What am I really afraid of?" "What's the worst thing that can happen?" "What am I unsure of?" "Where are these feelings coming from?" "Are they facts or thoughts?" "Do these feelings exist only in me because I feed them, or are these real things that are holding me back?" Name it all in concrete terms, not vague generalizations. What has to happen to stop being fearful and uncertain? What can you undertake to do something about it?

The quality of your questions very much determines the quality of your life. Well-focused questions provide insight and clarity. It's about questioning further. The answer to your first question is always a prompt for a follow-up question. Do this calmly, and take your time. And make sure that you're in a positive state of mind; otherwise, you'll be weighed down by a negative mindset before you even start. Keep digging. The moment will come when you suddenly have clarity. All the answers are already there. It's up to you to ask the right questions.

Examples of good questions:

- What can I learn from this?
- Why do I do what I do?
- Why am I spending time on this?
- What can I do to improve myself?
- What can go wrong, and what can I do to prevent that?
- Who can help me with this?
- What do I need in order to … ?
- What is the next step to … ?
- What is my (unique) added value?
- What do I have to offer?
- Why am I asking this question?
- What do I really want to know?
- What do I really mean by this?

Here's a story from one of my coaching sessions. Rose wanted to start her own company. She was 34 and truly radiant. A motivated, enthusiastic woman, she had a clear vision and was a pleasure to listen to. Her communication skills had helped her become a successful sales consultant. She figured she'd earned her spurs and now wanted to venture out on her own. She knew exactly what she wanted, knew what she was good at, and had done her homework. In a few coaching sessions, I'd helped her on her way, and Rose was determined to leave her job.

Yet from the moment she'd enthusiastically shared her plans with her friends and parents, she was inundated with warnings and well-meaning advice. "If I were you, I wouldn't do it—imagine it doesn't work out." Her parents thought it was extremely foolish of her to give up the security of a good salary, especially since Rose had just bought a house. A trusted friend thought it was a substantial risk. He knew someone who'd tried to start his own business, and that had gone completely down the drain.

After hearing, "What if things go wrong?" for the umpteenth time, Rose was confused. Her vivaciousness had evaporated. After a deep sigh, she said, "I don't know. I only hear disastrous stories about failure and people ending up in financial trouble. Who says I'll have enough clients, and what if it really doesn't work out?"

"Rose, why are you letting them bring you down? Where's that energetic go-getter, that conqueror? Where's the real Rose? Have you stopped believing in yourself?" She looked at me, sighed, and said nothing, but her eyes reflected her dejectedness. "They know you better than I do. Maybe they're right. Don't do it, better for everyone, problem solved," I said.

"What do you mean, don't do it?" Like a phoenix, she arose from her own ashes. I started asking her questions. What did she and that failed entrepreneur have in common? Perhaps that person wasn't cut out to be an entrepreneur, not convinced in his abilities and not competent. Or maybe he didn't have a well-thought-out plan. She didn't know what the circumstances were; his failure could have had all kinds of causes. "On the other hand, why would you not continue doing what you do now? You earn almost three times the average. Why would you give up that certainty?"

She'd thought about that. It was one of the reasons she wanted to start her own company. Rose felt several of her colleagues lacked commitment. And she had to comply with so many company rules that she no longer felt free. She wanted that freedom back, preferably with a number of great colleagues whom she could choose herself.

In the sessions that followed, we analyzed the behavior of the people around her and the notions upon which they'd based their well-meaning advice. The trusted friend turned out to be quite a white-picket-fence type. Was it any wonder he'd advised against it? Rose's parents weren't entrepreneurs. Their reaction was understandable, but on what grounds could they judge that Rose quitting her job would be unwise? Some girlfriends thought it sounded exciting, although they wouldn't be quick to do it themselves.

Were these people really capable of advising others when it came to entrepreneurship? And what did all this say about Rose? In my opinion, she needed a few new entrepreneurial friends, people who inspired her and could expertly advise her.

Bad advice is given free of charge but has little value. Bad arguments are both plentiful and useless. What's more, they can make you insecure. Rose, a strong woman who wasn't easily deterred, had been scared off because she'd started focusing all her attention on potential problems and failure. Her brain had gone to work on the question "What if things go wrong?" Subsequently, she started entertaining every possible negative eventuality.

Do you recognize this? Then you can do one of two things: gather more worthless opinions to feed your negative thinking or seek valuable advice from professionals and specialists.

By formulating more focused questions, you can ask good, constructive ones. What could go wrong? This is the subject of your research. Then ask yourself: "What can I do to prevent this from happening?" "Who can help me in that case?" "Are there other unwelcome scenarios?" By considering these questions carefully, you can avoid many potential problems and be prepared for setbacks. Do remember that there can always be situations that you can't foresee. Never underestimate how wrong you can be.

> *"To find out what you want,*
> *it's important to know who you are.*
> *It's a big life question: Who are you?"*

Discovering Who You Really Are

Who are you? Answering that question is one of the most important challenges of our existence. And it is not easy. It is a journey that you travel. The road to your true self, discovering more and more about yourself is not something that just happens. As if one day you will have the answer and you will have learned it all at once. It takes time, usually a lot of time. And every time you think you know yourself completely, you will discover a new side to explore.

You change as you grow older and experience things. New dreams and new goals emerge. You gain more experience and learn life lessons. And you become increasingly aware of your behavior and self-image. Of your way of thinking and of how you look at the world. During this search for yourself, you discover what you find important and what you stand for. You become increasingly aware of certain sides and characteristics of yourself. This allows you to better understand your own behavior and possibly change it.

How Would You Describe Yourself?

If I asked you who you are, what would you say? I'm not talking about your name. Or what you do and who your friends are. Or what clothes you wear and how you show yourself to the outside world and on social media. Although those things have to do with it because they say something about what you think is important. Who you are as a person goes far beyond a description of your age, work, family, and interests.

Here's an example. Richard introduced himself to me: "I'm Richard, I'm 37 years old, the father of two children, and happily married. I work as a nurse in the children's ward of a hospital. In my spare time, I help volunteer at my children's school and at their sports club, and my dream is to take a year-long trip around the world with my family."

What do you now know about who Richard is? The first few things tell us something about his social status, the labels we give ourselves, the roles we play. With this, you can picture Richard in your mind, but what does that say about his emotions and inner world? What do you now know about his personality?

Your personality is the set of qualities that describe how you think, how you react to others and situations, what motivates you, and the emotions that characterize you. The term "personality" is derived from the Latin *persona*. It means "mask," the role you play, the character you take on. It has to do with your external behavior. Your personality is influenced by your upbringing and your environment, by the people you spend time with. Research shows that as you grow older, your personality changes as a result of life events and the meaning you assign to those events.

You Are Not Just the Way You Are

Sometimes you hear people say, "It's just the way I am." That is nonsense. You're not just the way you are. It's largely your own choice. Not entirely, because your height is not a choice, but your weight often is. If you are overweight due to eating too much unhealthy food, too much booze, too much sugar, and too little exercise, it is usually the result of your own choices. Whether you look well-groomed or not is a choice. Whether your house is tidy or a mess is a choice. Whether you fail exams because you haven't studied, whether you are almost always late, often oversleep, or forget things. None of that is because that's who you are.

Yes, there are things you have little or no control over. Think about your genes or the country you were born in. You may face adversity or illness. Possibly a medical condition over which you have little or no control. But those things don't define who you are and who you become. What matters is how you deal with those circumstances.

And that has to do with your personality and your mindset. What kind of person are you? A go-getter or a quitter? Do you believe in yourself or are you insecure? Are you enterprising? Are you a hard worker or lazy? How you are and what you do is your own choice and responsibility.

Personal Values

To get to know yourself better, you need to identify your personal values because these form the basis of your personality and behavior. What are your personal values? What do you think is important? If you value freedom, independence, and self-reliance, a nine-to-five office job is unlikely to contribute to your happiness. But if security is important to you, then that office job can mean comfort, convenience, and peace of mind. You are less likely to take risks and prefer to follow all the rules. You find a secure job more important than an exciting and adventurous life with an uncertain future. You know what you have, you never know what you will get. The work itself may not bring you satisfaction, but it can provide you with a fixed monthly income and leave you with free time for yourself in the evenings and on the weekends.

Everyone has personal values. But what they are and in what order you prioritize them varies from person to person. At the top of my list are freedom and independence. Also important are health, money, inner peace, caring, gratitude, and loving consciousness. Loving consciousness is more than just love as you feel it for someone. It is a state of being. I try to deal with other people, animals, and nature in a loving way as much as possible. Loving consciousness means that I have the good for others. Gratitude, caring, and kindness all has to do with that way of life.

Independence is so high on my list of personal values because I think it is important to organize my time myself. I need to decide what I do and when I do it. Now I must honestly admit that in practice with running three companies this is not always quite so, because I have committed myself to responsibilities and work. And when you make commitments, you have to stick to them. I always will, because responsibility is also an important value for me.

To live the way I want, sufficient money is needed. A free and independent life comes with a price tag. Therefore, money has been an important personal value all my life. But freedom outweighs money. When I sold my media company, I was offered a substantial salary to continue working in a high position, now as an employee of a publicly traded company. But money was less important to me than my freedom and independence. An office job with long meetings and political games is not for me. That job was not in line with my personal values. It would not have made me happy.

Getting to Know Yourself Better

There's a reason behind every choice you make. There are reasons why you decide to do or not do something, and those reasons chart your course. In other words, the meaning you assign to your thoughts determines your personality, your behavior, how you feel, how you react, and what you accomplish. Everything you do has a reason. If you are struggling in a relationship, you can decide to break up, or you can turn it into a protracted drama that lasts for years. And there's a reason you choose one or the other. As you will notice, there is a close relationship between your personal values and the choices you make. And this all directly affects your behavior.

Perhaps a good salary or a high management position gives you a feeling of being important. So, you care about prestige and status above all else.

Or you are concerned with recognition. To be seen and to belong, to get approval from others. This can mean an enormous urge to prove yourself, or behaving in ways that you think will please others. The latter is also possible if caring is your driving force. You will do a lot for others. Perhaps even so much that you start pleasing others too much and forget to please or to take care of yourself. Practice shows that this invariably leads to mental problems or even burnout, because you start living the way you think others expect you to.

The pleaser cancels themself out and does as much as possible to be liked. As a result, it can feel as if you are neither appreciated nor seen. But you do not really dare to make yourself visible. You prefer to avoid discussions and conflicts. And you are reluctant to say what bothers you.

Someone with a desire to prove themself wants to be the center of attention. So, this is also about recognition. The hard worker, who talks a lot, enters into discussions to be right. And does everything to get confirmation: I am doing well.

I have some more questions for you. Why do you wear the clothes you wear? Because you like them? Because they fit who you want to be? Or do you consider how others will look at you then? Why do you wear one brand and not another? Why do you prefer a certain car brand? What is your political preference? Do your posts on social media reflect reality or a fantasy world?

Why do you make these choices? Why do you do what you do? And what do you find important? These are good questions to think about, because the answers tell a lot about you.

Now is the question: Do you really know what you mean by all your answers? Therefore, you have to go deeper into that and ask yourself each time: "What do I really mean by this?" Because the point is to understand yourself better and better.

Taking it a step further, I can talk about my outlook on life, the world, and what affects me. What emotions come to me in certain situations, my feelings and thoughts. For example, I can't stand injustice. It makes me angry and spurs something in me to fight for justice. In this way, also dig into yourself to find out what is really going on inside you and what propels you to take the actions you do. Because if you can probe your thoughts and emotions, then you can understand yourself.

Personal Values Shape Your Behavior

Do you see how your personal values have a lot of influence on your behavior and the choices you make? In the same way, you can trace your behavior and your choices back to your personal values. But these can sometimes be somewhat buried away.

One of my clients, a very wealthy lady, was saving a few hundred dollars a month by not hiring a housekeeper, even though she had a 14-room house. She did go shopping regularly: a new Louis Vuitton bag here, a pair of Gucci shoes there, a Valentino dress for her daughter. We talked about what she considered important, her personal values.

If you looked at her spending habits, you'd think that time was of less value to her because she preferred spending two days cleaning her huge house herself to paying someone $1,000 a month to take that work off her hands. She could easily afford it. And it turned out she really didn't like cleaning either. She did, however, easily and regularly spend thousands of dollars on luxury items. What personal values of hers were behind this?

These chic gifts made her daughter happy, she said. "Giving" made her feel good, and she hoped to get appreciation and recognition from her daughter in return. The two had conflicts regularly, and the daughter didn't always hold her mother in high regard. Because the mother expected, or at least hoped for, a bit of attention and love in return, the "giving" was also a bit of "trading."

Why did she spend thousands of dollars on expensive bags, clothes, and shoes for herself? It was part of her lifestyle (habit); she really found them beautiful. It made her feel good. I asked her why she wouldn't buy a nice bag for 50 bucks or a pair of shoes for a hundred dollars. That wouldn't suit her, she said, although she did have to think about that question for a moment. Did it not suit who she was or who she wanted to be to the outside world?

As her coach I knew her personal situation well, and I understood her way of thinking, which explained her behavior. Her personal values included recognition, appreciation, and prestige. She wanted to be seen and liked while also wanting to set her limits, and she preferred to stay out of the limelight. In practice, this invariably led to internal conflicts. She regularly received compliments on the beautiful things she wore but was also sometimes criticized for spending so much money. But she could now say she was also very frugal because she did the housework herself.

Personal values are things that you place great value on, both positive and negative. Your positive personal values, in particular, are a reflection of who you are or want to be. These values unconsciously form guidelines. They guide the choices you make, how you deal with others, and how you relate to society. They explain why you do what you do.

Suppose recognition, appreciation, service, and kindness are especially important to you—you want to be liked—and you don't like rejection and disagreement; then it's quite possible you'll tend to neglect your own needs in favor of another's. As a result, your self-esteem plays second fiddle. But if self-esteem is simultaneously an important personal value for you, you'll end up with an internal conflict.

I'll give you a few more examples of conflicting values that lead to inner turmoil. You want to earn a lot of money, but you're not willing to work hard and sacrifice your free time. You prefer to have fun now, and you don't want to be too preoccupied with "later" just yet.

Your friends invite you to go hang gliding, a powerful experience of freedom that's in line with your personal values of adventure and freedom. On the other hand, you also like security and don't want to take big risks.

To gain the appreciation of others, you talk a lot, want to impress, and are a little too emphatic. This can go against your other important personal values of sincerity, honesty, inner peace, integrity, connection, and therefore, appreciation.

When you discover such an internal conflict in yourself, it's important to figure out which values weigh more heavily and what you can do to resolve the conflict. Suppose you've written down health as an important personal value, but in practice, you don't really eat healthy—well, then you're just fooling yourself. Write down what you eat over the course of a week, for example. That can be a first step toward change.

The value that is most important to you is what I call your driving force. It gives direction to your existence and guides most of the choices you make. Think about it. What could be your driving force?

Whenever you need to make a choice from now on, take out the list of your personal values and see whether the choice you want to make is in line with what matters to you. Then check your personal values against the goals you've set for yourself. The goals you want to achieve and the dreams you want to fulfill have to be in harmony with your personal values. If they're not, or if you aren't completely honest about those personal values you've written down, then chances are extremely slim you'll get the results you're looking for.

It can also be helpful in relationships to know about each other and what the other's personal values are. The beginning of most relationships is a happy time, but for the long term, it's crucial to know your and your partner's underlying personal values. If you value modesty, prefer to stay in the background, and don't care much about status and success, then a relationship with someone who likes to be front and center and wants a lot of attention from others may not always be the best match. Someone who values lots of downtime won't necessarily be a good match for someone for whom hard work is important. These are easy-to-grasp examples, but things get considerably more complex when someone's behavior (or your own) can't be immediately explained.

Then it makes sense to examine the values underpinning the behavior.

When you start observing the people around you without judgment, observing how they behave and why they behave that way, you can figure out what their personal values may be. Of course, it matters much more that you understand what your own values are, but observing others attentively can give you some rather good insights.

If you're able to be very honest with yourself, you can go ahead and write down your list of personal values. In practice, however, you'll notice that you're often tempted to stray from those values because they can lead to (internal) dilemmas or conflicts. As a result, you adjust your behavior, and from there, you may find yourself moving further and further away from your personal values. This is what often happens when you have low self-esteem, or when connection with others outweighs all else for you. You then try to avoid conflict and do things "for the sake of peace." You try to please others to get attention and appreciation. Because you soon neglect your own needs, you fade into the background, out of the light and into the dark. What you're actually doing in those moments is taking yourself out of the game; you become a bystander, a pawn for others.

Personal values don't remain the same throughout your life. They'll evolve over the years. This has to do with what you go through as a person as well as how you see the world and the way you fit into it. They form the basis for the choices you make. So, if you want to get to know yourself, it's important to spend time on identifying and understanding your personal values and paying attention to them.

There are both positive and negative personal values. You could say, these are values that you like to attract to you. But there are also negative values. Then it is about something you do not want. Often it is something that bothers you, or something you find annoying in yourself or in other people. A negative value is something you prefer to keep at a distance. Examples include laziness, negligence, frustration, manipulation, abuse of power, and dishonesty.

Now write down your positive and negative personal values, and then rank them. It's about what you think is important, what you value.

Take at least a half an hour for this assignment when you do it the first time. Review it the next day, and then repeatedly thereafter. In the first few weeks, you'll move things on your list around or might even make big changes to it. After a while, you'll really be able to see yourself in the values you've put down for yourself. Then it will just feel right.

Assignment

What are your 10–15 most important positive personal values? Rank the one that is most important with a 1, and then the rest in descending order.

Suggestions: adventure, ambition, appearance, being happy, being of service, certainty, comfort, confidence, connection, contributing to society, convenience, courtesy, creativity, discipline, ease, empathy, enthusiasm, family, financial independence, freedom, friendliness, friendship, gratitude, health, honesty, independence, inner peace, integrity, intimacy, joy, justice, leadership, learning (knowledge), love, loyalty, luxury, modesty, money, passion, peace, peace of mind, perfection, personal growth, pleasure, prestige, recognition, relationships, relaxation, reliability, religion, resourcefulness, respect, satisfaction, self-esteem, spirituality, status, success, thoughtfulness, tolerance, vitality, wisdom, work, wealth.

What are your most significant negative personal values? Rank the one that is most significant with a 1 (the one you find most annoying), and then the rest in descending order.

Suggestions: addiction, anger, anguish, anxiety, arrogance, being critical of others, boredom, depression, disagreeability, dishonesty, doubt, failure, envy, fear, frustration, guilt, impatience, jealousy, procrastination, laziness, loneliness, lying, manipulation, meddlesomeness, melancholy, naivety, neglect, not taking responsibility, rejection, sadness, selfishness, taking too much responsibility, tendency to generalize, uncertainty, (unnecessary) worry.

Your Personal Statute

You can complement your list of personal values by writing down your personal statute, a kind of regulation that is, in principle, always in effect. These are the rules that you draw up for yourself and hold yourself to as a result. They describe who and what you want to be (your personality) and what you want to do.

Stephen Covey explains the importance of the personal statute in *The 7 Habits of Highly Effective People*. It's one of the most effective ways to improve the quality of your life. It forms the basis of personal leadership, and it also appears to be an important way to prevent burnout and related illnesses.

If you don't have your own personal rules that guide you, how do you know how you should live your daily life? Without rules, how do you know what you should and shouldn't do? And it is up to you to make these rules. Most people have no idea; that's why their lives get complicated or confused. But when you have clear rules about what you want and don't want, rules that form a constitution for your life, your life gets much easier.

A personal statute gives shape and substance to your existence. It is the basis upon which you can test your decisions and choices, such as how you spend your time and how you deal with things. You can also rely on it when you're confused by your emotions or when you can't think clearly anymore. It serves as the guide for your life.

The writing process forces you to think carefully about your priorities and align your behavior with your personal values. Abiding by your statute is even more important than writing it down.

This philosophy isn't something you jot down in an hour. You'll have to examine your innermost self in detail in order to sketch an accurate self-image. You'll write, scrap, and rewrite until you feel everything's right. It can take days or weeks, but it's definitely worth the effort. It's about the quality of your daily life and how you give meaning to your existence. Because your thinking and insights will change as you age due to changing life circumstances and other reasons, you'll also want to reexamine and perhaps rewrite your personal statute over time.

I describe my own life philosophy extensively in this book. It would be useful for you to write down a short version of your own so you can read it every day, or at least once every few days. You could also write a letter to yourself with recommendations on how you want to live your life and the rules you need to follow as a result. Here, too, the act of simply writing it down will get you thinking. More importantly, the daily or weekly reading of your own life rules will lead to your personal success and the life you want to live.

To give you an example, I'd like to share part of my personal statute with you.

My Personal Values

1. Freedom and independence
2. Health and vitality
3. Inner peace
4. Loving awareness
5. Wisdom and spiritual growth

6. Gratitude
7. Financial and professional success
8. Aesthetics
9. Responsibility
10. Making a contribution to society

My Personal Rules

- I am the result of the way I think.
- I am the result of the choices I make.
- I take responsibility for my actions.
- I live my life based on my own rules.
- I live and eat healthy.
- I spend time on and pay attention to my mental and physical health every day.
- I do not allow my feelings of happiness to be diminished by circumstances, setbacks, the criticism of others, or people who express themselves negatively.
- I am financially independent and do not spend my money irresponsibly.
- I support the people I love, including financially if necessary.
- I give attention and love to the people I care about.
- I feel connected to Cosmic Intelligence.
- I have trust that I am being guided.
- I judge as little as possible and observe as purely as possible.
- I live from a place of love.
- I live from a place of trust.
- I ask experts for advice.
- I make use of my talents.
- I try to learn something from everyone and every situation.
- I help others improve the quality of their lives.
- I help people in need.
- I regularly do something charitable.

- I am committed to making a daily contribution to a peaceful, healthy, tolerant, loving, and happy society.
- I take time for myself to maintain an overview of what I am doing.
- I regularly take time for myself to find peace and quiet.
- I am grateful every day and express my gratitude every day.
- I ask myself this every day: What about myself can I improve?
- I enjoy every day.

Stay True to Your Rules of Life

A lot of people adapt their behavior to their environment, especially to gain recognition and appreciation. Or they're led by how others want them to behave. And in most cases, behavior is a consequence of conditioning, the convictions you've come to accept as your truth. Such people don't stick to their personal values. To not lose yourself and, on the contrary, to remain true to yourself, it is very important that you stick to your own rules. It is your constitution, your handhold, on which you can always rely.

> *"True happiness doesn't come from what we have,*
> *but from who we are."*

Happiness Is a State of Mind

This part of the book delved into the philosophy of happiness and success. Fulfillment and happiness arise from discovering the mysteries of life. You may accumulate wealth and impress others with your lifestyle, but if you don't seek to understand the true essence of life, you'll be left feeling empty and unhappy inside.

"One sees clearly only with the heart. What is essential is invisible to the eye," wrote Antoine de Saint-Exupéry in *The Little Prince*, one of my favorite books. As long as we view the world only through our eyes and not through our hearts, we will not find peace. The highest form of happiness is to love. What else but love can give meaning to our lives?

Live from a place of love, and you will feel happiness. Love holds no judgment; love simply is. Love purifies, diminishes pain and troubles, and encompasses everything. If you close your eyes and open your heart, your thoughts disappear. In that moment, you are centered in your heart and see only love. We try to see love with our eyes, but it's impossible; only our heart can see love. Let go of your thoughts, be present in this moment, and let everything be as it is. That is love.

True happiness doesn't stem from what we possess but from who we are. This feeling is the result of personal and spiritual growth, which is why some people feel unhappy. They have stopped growing, and anything that ceases to grow slowly withers. It either grows or it dies. So, when your mind becomes stuck in old habits, clinging to the past, it creates the perfect conditions for an unhappy existence.

Happiness means being in alignment and harmony with yourself. It's not something you can own or hold onto; it's an experience and an attitude toward life. The desire for happiness is universal, and the path to it always lies within ourselves. It's a fundamental need, something everyone longs for, yet it's unrealistic to expect to feel happy all the time. A constant state of happiness is unachievable. If you chase it relentlessly, it will only lead to suffering. But if you change your thoughts, suffering can dissolve, leaving happiness in its place. Like a sculptor who doesn't create what he finds beautiful but carves away what overshadows the beauty of his masterpiece.

If you truly want to experience happiness and achieve success, you need to gain a deep understanding of your thinking mind and thought patterns.

We are here on earth to bring a bit more light, warmth, and humanity into the world. We're here to fulfill a purpose, which can take on any form. Each of us can be a light in someone else's darkness. While we aren't responsible for the whole world, we are responsible for the world around us—and, most importantly, for ourselves.

How do you view your responsibility? Is your life as it is today shaped by your own creation, or has it unfolded without your influence? Of course, we all face external situations and influences. But it's not the situations themselves that are defining; rather, it's how you respond to them. Who you are now and where you stand is a result of all the choices you've made so far—or the ones you didn't make because you were afraid to choose. Perhaps you have a well-paying job and a loving relationship. You live with your partner and children in a cozy home, with a nice car parked in the driveway. You draw inspiration from interesting books and share your life's joy with close friends. You have enough savings, and you take family trips to explore new places a few times a year. Or maybe you've been searching endlessly for that perfect relationship, feeling unfulfilled at work, lacking love and appreciation, struggling with finances, and unable to achieve your goals. Life feels against you, full of misfortune, and seemingly hopeless.

Many people complicate their lives unnecessarily. Remember, life is too short to suffer. Pain, misfortune, sadness, and tragedy are all part of life, but how you handle them is a choice. You can choose to be a victim of circumstances, or you can take responsibility and steer your own life. There are people who live in truly difficult circumstances, in situations they can't easily change. In such cases, it is the responsibility of those in more fortunate parts of the world to offer help, acting out of love and compassion.

I also see many people around me who are unable to experience true happiness. This requires a certain level of consciousness. Being aware of what is happening within your inner world is the key to happiness, and that same key unlocks inner peace and freedom.

Your behavior and the choices you make are directly tied to your personal values. These values differ for everyone, which is why it's essential to have a crystal-clear understanding of what your values are and why they are important to you. By combining these values with your personal mission statement, and considering any limiting beliefs you may hold (which we'll explore in the next part), you will gain a deeper understanding of your own behavior. You'll come to realize how your mindset has taken shape and that you hold the key to access your most fulfilling life.

The Keys to Mastering Your Mindset

- **Live your best life:** Happiness and success stem from simplicity, spiritual growth, love, and gratitude. Maintain balance among your material world, physical health, and the inner spiritual world.
- **Success beyond material wealth:** While money doesn't guarantee happiness, financial stability can remove stress and open doors to more fulfilling experiences. Yet true success is defined by wisdom, freedom, inner peace, love, and meaningful relationships, not just money.
- **Preparation meets opportunity:** Those who are prepared for opportunities are more likely to experience success and "good fortune."

- **Thoughts create reality:** Your beliefs and thoughts shape your life. You become what you believe, not what you merely wish for.
- **Mindset drives success:** A positive mental attitude and resilience are key to overcoming challenges and achieving long-term success and happiness. Pursuing what you love with passion and determination aligns both spiritual and material success.
- **Clear thinking through mindfulness:** Clear thinking comes from taking time to reflect, meditate, and create space for your mind to quiet and find answers.
- **Adapt to life's seasons:** Life has cycles of challenge and growth. Learn to adapt and find opportunities even in difficult times.
- **Inner peace enables clarity and brings fulfillment:** Silence and meditation allow you to connect with higher consciousness, offering clarity and helping you make wiser decisions. Continuous self-improvement and aligning your life with personal values bring a deeper sense of contentment and joy.
- **Power of asking the right questions:** Asking good, focused questions leads to clarity, better decision-making, and greater self-understanding, ultimately guiding you toward success.
- **Life is a journey, not a destination:** Life's path is shaped by the choices you make, and it's important to define your direction while allowing room for adventure.

*"You believe in your own story.
That story is your reality.
And it is that reality that determines
your vision of the world and the results you get."*

PART

III

Master Your Mindset

Your Personal Operating System

EVERYTHING HAPPENS WITHIN you. You look around you, at the outside world, but your experience of things takes place in your inner world. How you experience your life takes place in your own thoughts. That is the mind's playing field.

Your mind is your mental operating system. It determines who you are, what you do, how you think, and how you experience the world. A thought arises out of nowhere, and then an internal dialogue generally starts up. This internal discussion begins with that one thought. The meaning you assign to any given thought, event, or situation determines everything: your mindset, your view of reality, and how you react to and act on it.

At the beginning of the last century, the Indian spiritual leader Krishnamurti said, "Whether we are capitalists, socialists, Buddhists, Christians, Muslims, Black, White, or Brown, we are humans. What makes us different is how we think, our social conditioning, our traditions, and our beliefs, religious or not; it is the belief we have in our own reality."

And this was not only true in the previous century. It's what you also see very clearly in our present world, especially lately. Everyone lives in their own reality. Everyone believes in their own truth.

This is the most important part of this book. If virtually everything is the result of your mindset, it's high time you mastered it. This starts with insight into how your programming—your thought patterns and beliefs—came to be. In science, programming is also called a paradigm: a complex set of views, a frame of reference through which you interpret the world around you. It's a filter through which you take in, color, and organize information. We all experience the world around us through our own unique filters. Your filter forms your frame of mind and, therefore, the reality in which you believe. It's your own personal reality.

You could compare it to your social media timeline. Yours wouldn't look like mine. You and I see different messages in our feeds. You have different friends and messages than I do, and different people comment on them. We might see the same messages once in a while if we share some interests or network. Our lives are happening at the same time, yet the content you get on Facebook, LinkedIn, or Instagram is totally different than mine. No two timelines are the same, just as no two people are.

Similarly, every individual has been programmed over the years through their own conditioning.

You now know that by asking questions, you can gain insight into the way you've been unconsciously programmed. This awareness is absolutely vital to being able to master your mindset. In this part of the book, I'll go into this in much more detail, and I'll share with you how you can change your thought patterns and personal programming permanently and for the better.

It's fairly easy to understand how programming works and how you create thought patterns by comparing yourself to a new computer without an operating system. The hard disk and working memory start out empty. From the moment you come to life, every impression streaming in from outside gets stored. That process begins in the womb and accelerates after your birth. In your younger years in particular, you operate from a pure state of consciousness because you don't yet have any experiences you can refer to. All the information you receive and all the things you hear, see, feel, and experience get saved.

Your hard drive (your subconscious mind) gradually fills with hundreds of thousands of stored files (experiences, learning moments, information, feelings, and thoughts) and new software programs (skills). This whole forms your frame of reference, and your personal operating system starts to form on the basis of this. You can think of it as programming that's made up of countless thought patterns and an accumulation of habits.

You receive both correct and incorrect information, but you can't differentiate between what gets stored. Your system contains bugs, and as a result, your hard drive has been programmed with a plethora of incorrect data. Again and again, new corrupt files and viruses penetrate the realm of the hard disk, yet you're so convinced of your own truth that you don't notice it.

What happens when there are bugs in a computer's operating system? They need to be worked out, but deviating from what's been programmed can be tough. As soon as you start to do that, the system does everything it can to bring things back in line. You have to break through this resistance to be able to deal with the bugs in your operating system. You have to identify and repair the root cause. Your conditioning is the mental equivalent of this, and it has near-exclusive control over your behavior, how you think, what you do, how you react to things, and how you feel.

Because your thinking has such far-reaching consequences, it's crucial that you understand how things work in your head, especially if you want to change something in your life or achieve certain goals. You can't do that without taking a deep dive into your own programming and making changes to it.

The takeaway here is this: if you continue to do what you've always done, you'll continue to get the same results. In other words, if the way you've done something hasn't worked, it makes no sense to do it again in exactly the same way, because there's a good chance you'll get the same result. Something in the formula, in the way you approach things, has to change. It's a matter of being fully aware of what you do and discovering what you should change in order to get a different outcome. If what you've changed doesn't work, keep tweaking things until you get a different result. Keep changing and fine-tuning your approach until you get the results you want. In other words, if you want to change something about yourself, your behavior, or your existence, you'll have to rewrite your story, overhaul your operating system. And you can't just merely believe this new story; you have to be really and deeply convinced of it.

How many times have you planned to do something and failed? Losing weight, quitting smoking, learning a language, studying more, being more caring and understanding toward your partner, drinking less alcohol, exercising more, taking a daily meditation moment, reading an hour a day, taking more time for yourself, saving money, getting started on making your dream come true. If you want these things so much, why haven't you done them yet?

Reason 1: Because your operating system isn't currently allowing it. The programming doesn't want to be overwritten. It wants to protect you from extra effort and possible failure. So, it will make you believe that you should not take a risk to change. This is a long-lasting, deeply ingrained pattern you're dealing with. That old pattern is like a five-lane highway; it's easy-breezy. Forming a new pattern is like carving out an entirely new path through a forest. It certainly won't be easy to traverse at first.

Reason 2: Because you don't really want it. You act like you do, but you're only fooling yourself. You're unable to reprogram your hard drive because you lack the desire, the burning platform, the self-discipline, the perseverance, and the willpower to do so. Because if you really want something, you'll do what needs to be done—unapologetically, without bitching, and without making excuses.

When you really want something, you're prepared to do whatever it takes, even when it seems impossible or demands a lot of you. That's when you really want something. The desire must be huge, or there must be necessity, because then you have to. But in most cases, we don't have the self-discipline and drop out prematurely, or don't even start. If you recognize yourself in this, do not expect success or rewards, because these are only granted to people who give their all.

In recent years, I have experienced many people who, after reading my books and following my programs, have made radical decisions to live their best lives. These people suddenly realized that it's a deliberate, well-thought-out choice. They also understood what the negative consequences would be if they didn't rigorously change course. In doing so, they created a need within themselves, which gives them the willpower to do it.

You have to ruthlessly break through your thought patterns and habitual behaviors. The point is that it takes almost no effort if you really want something. So, the question is: How badly do you want it? Is it a need? The choice is yours whether to take action or not. It's entirely your responsibility.

Wishing and hoping are the stuff of fairy tales. Wishing and wanting are not enough. A lot of people want a lot, but precious little generally comes of it. Transform your "I want" into "I must!" Because if you must, you will.

Where Do Your Convictions Come From?

"You believe what you want to believe, and you always find something to confirm your own reality. That's how strong the power of your thoughts is."

Thoughts are the muscles of the mind. If your thought patterns have been in incorrect alignment for a long time, it'll take time and training to make them flexible again and be able to mold them into what you want.

The creation of thought patterns is often an unconscious process. You don't notice it. Where do your convictions come from? How did they end up in you? You need to understand how that operating system has shaped itself and how those thought patterns define your life. Only then can you have control over your life.

To fully understand this part on thought patterns and mastering your mindset, it's important that you understand the distinction between body and mind. According to many scientists and researchers, the mind, with its thoughts, is a product of the brain, a fabrication of our own making. They made the conclusion that the mind is the result of our hundred billion brain cells.

This proposition seems plausible to me, especially given the fact they are experts. Based on my own experience, I see the mind as an energy field found in every cell of the body, including the brain, and believe this energy field is also in motion outside our physical body. Your body is just a small part of who you are, an instrument for your vast mind, which consists of your limited consciousness and the infinitely large subconscious. This view is reflected in many ancient philosophies and spiritual approaches, and I've never heard a convincing argument that disproves it.

You receive information through your senses. When that information has been processed by your brain, you become aware of it. This is your consciousness, the part of the mind that thinks and rationalizes. This is also where your free will resides, the power to choose. The conscious mind can accept or reject any idea or thought, while the subconscious cannot. Just like a hard drive, it allows everything in and can't distinguish between good and bad, reality and imagination. It doesn't judge; it is. All those thoughts, emotions, images, and experiences leave traces behind in your subconscious mind. Remember the weeds in the flower garden. Negative thoughts are the weeds of your mind. If you don't get rid of them right away, they'll grow wild and deprive you of perspective.

You do that weeding by consciously choosing what you focus on. The thoughts you pay the most attention to affect your daily life. If you remain stuck in negative, angry, insecure, and anxious thoughts, you won't move forward. Positive, inspiring, cheerful, and successful thoughts, on the other hand, receive the reward of happiness, inner peace, freedom, money, and a beautiful life. When you repeat a thought over and over again, you begin to believe in that thought. Saying that thought out loud reinforces your programming. This predominant thought then becomes automated, a habit, regardless of whether it helps or hurts you. But beware, I do not mean simply positive thinking and certainly not pretending that everything is rosy in one situation or experience will get your results. Rather, a positive mental attitude is a state of being, a way of life.

The subconscious is driven by the programming you have done yourself and the programming that was done without your being aware of it. It expresses itself in how you feel, how you react, and what you do. If you create predominantly negative thoughts, they immediately influence your behavior and emotions, and ultimately, what you achieve. Do you put healthy fruits and vegetables in the blender, or alcohol, drugs, and antidepressants? Are you creating a beneficial blend, or a toxic cocktail? The outcome depends on the recipe and ingredients. That's how it also works with thoughts. The learning process of being positive (which is more than only thinking that way) begins with the recognition of destructive thoughts. Once you become aware that your negative thoughts lead to negative emotions, you can replace them with positive thoughts.

The Quality of Your Life

What determines the quality of your life? Your education, your job, your relationship, your health, your network, your friends, how much money you have, economic circumstances, your freedom? All these elements can be of influence, but the quality of your life is largely determined by your thoughts and emotions.

Emotions give us the strength to accomplish exceptional things, both positive and negative. Endless aspirations can make you invincible. But people also put their reputation on the line when they cannot control their desires. Powerlessness and the loss of a loved one can drive one to despair. Overpowering emotion can cause people to lose their senses and become destructive or, alternatively, rise above themselves and perform heroic acts. Your experience of something is determined by the emotions you feel about the event. Those emotions color your thoughts and shape your reality. Does that sound a bit abstract?

How you deal with an event or situation completely determines the action you take. What happens to your emotions when you ask yourself confusing questions? Do you keep ruminating on why you didn't do something differently? Or why all this happened to you, that it wasn't fair, that you didn't deserve it? Whatever you focus your attention on will grow until you become completely entangled in your flights of fancy.

Did something bad happen to you in the past? Perhaps you were bullied at school, for example. That can't be changed now. The only thing you can change is the meaning you assign to it, the way you deal with it. Are you still being bullied now? That's generally not the case. Be aware of these things. Don't cling to "then," which is sometimes long ago. Don't keep putting yourself in the shoes of who you once were. This applies to all situations from the past that may still bother you today. Stay in the here and now in your consciousness. That's easier said than done, I know. But I also know that you can change your perception of that past. If it rained yesterday, you can't get wet from it today. Throw off the anchors of the past that are keeping you from moving forward. Enjoy what is there and don't make yourself unhappy with what isn't. If something's missing in your life, do something about it. If you think that's not possible, let it go. Either stop complaining and torturing yourself or do something and fill that void.

Sleepless nights and worrying about the future are not conducive to your peace of mind. In fact, focusing all your attention on a fictional scenario—a flight of fancy—over which you have no control will only drive you mad or make you afraid or angry. In fact, these kinds of twists of thought are in many instances negative. "Imagine this happens—then maybe ..." And another common one: "Do you have any idea of all the things that could go wrong?" This kind of doomsday thinking only immobilizes you, and the only thing that changes is how you experience it; the situation itself doesn't. It's pointless to worry about things you can't influence. See things for what they really are, and don't make them worse than they are.

Be aware of the issues you focus your attention on and the meaning you assign to situations, events, and your thoughts. The mind is not bound by time and can jump from the present to the past to the future at lightning speed. You can recall precious moments and dream about adventurous experiences, a new love, or business successes. During those thought journeys, you can also end up at the stations of pain, sorrow, regret, and anger. Or you can come up against doubt, uncertainty, worries, and fear.

Being mentally lost in time leads to unrest in your mind and body. Be aware of where you are, and focus your attention on the present. That doesn't mean you can't take a focused look back at the past or a glance forward into the future, as long as you don't get lost emotionally in false sentiments and a labyrinth of negative thought patterns.

> *"Mindsets are convictions.*
> *They are strong convictions,*
> *but it remains a way of thinking,*
> *and you can change your thinking."*
>
> **– Carol Dweck**

Static and Growth-Oriented Mindsets

To paraphrase what James Allen wrote in As a Man Thinketh, our minds are amazing instruments. With them, we can create symphonies when the conductor is competent enough to maintain harmony in the orchestra. The mind can also be a horrifying weapon, destroying countries and people. Every day, we navigate between these two extremes. Between them is every character trait, and humans are the creator and master of them. The thoughts we choose determine whether someone destroys themselves through those thoughts or chooses joy, peace, and strength. Our negative state of mind judges, is indifferent, and can be destructive. Our receptive mind is friendly, peaceful, and compassionate.

It is the eternal struggle between good and evil that resides within us. The way you've been conditioned, therefore, determines how you think, how you judge, and based on that, how you react and behave. There are two types of mindsets: positive and negative.

Psychology professor Carol Dweck makes a distinction between what she calls the "static" and the "growth-oriented" mindsets. This acclaimed Stanford University researcher in social and cognitive psychology has worked on matters of personal development, motivation, and intelligence for over 30 years. Her research has focused on the question of why some people are successful and others aren't. She shared her findings in her bestseller, *Mindset, The New Psychology of Success*.

Why is it that some people grow from setbacks and others are completely derailed by them? How is it that some people discover and make use of their talents and others don't? Why is it that some people struggle their whole lives and others end up as millionaires? These are some of the questions Dweck has wrestled with. Her studies are part of the so-called positive psychology movement. This movement is based on the power of people's convictions, on positive experiences (such as happiness, hope, and love), and positive characteristics (such as vitality, discipline, perseverance, and wisdom).

"Mindsets are convictions," says Dweck. "They are strong convictions, but it remains a way of thinking, and you can change your thinking." Based on years of research, she dares to state that intelligence and personal qualities are not innate, but largely the result of development and practice.

In *Mindset, The New Psychology of Success*, she also quotes Alfred Binet, the inventor of the IQ test. The test was created to find out whether children needed additional help, not determine their level of intelligence. Binet claimed that we can increase our acumen, our memory, our understanding, and the quality of our intelligence through practice, training, and repetition.

The positive (growth-oriented) mindset is about curiosity and being open to improvement. People with a positive attitude see opportunities and ask themselves how they can take advantage of them. People with a positive mindset figure out how they can improve themselves, their services, their products, and their environment. They see achieving their goal as a result of the learning process. They're mainly concerned with continuous learning and growth.

People with a static mindset believe that intelligence, personality, and character are immutable facts, that people are born that way, that those things can't be developed. From this perspective, you're either smart or stupid, talented or average. People with this mindset feel the need to prove themselves. They quickly—and wrongly—think that people negatively judge them. They often just quit when something isn't working, and then feel frustrated and rejected. They frequently have a negative self-image because they constantly compare themselves to others who are "better." They don't ask themselves what they could learn from those people. People with a predominantly static mindset want to maintain their acquired status as much as possible and avoid risks. They prefer to avoid new challenges that could threaten that position. If things go wrong when they undertake something, they won't readily admit that they were responsible, but instead blame someone else or the circumstances. This mindset and approach to life has a terribly negative impact on self-confidence and self-esteem.

Differences in mindset occur early on due to environmental factors: parents, family, friends, partners, and teachers. Conditioning is thus a decisive factor, but according to Dweck, the convictions you accept are ultimately a personal choice. Training and controlling your mind and mindset are the most important skills to master when you want to create and experience a successful and happy existence.

Intelligence, personality, and talents can grow through effort, commitment, and perseverance. According to Dweck's studies, this is how people with a growth-oriented mindset see things. They believe their potential is always greater than themselves. Therefore, these people also find it rewarding to seek out situations they can learn from. They dare to take responsibility and risks. And when something doesn't work out right away, they don't immediately feel powerless, desperate, and judged negatively by others. This attitude leads to greater resilience and stimulates them to put forth even greater effort.

You don't always have either a static or a growth-oriented mindset. One is always dominant, but in daily life, we navigate between the two extremes. Sometimes, your conditioning will make you very adamant (static) about something, while in another moment, you'll be receptive and open to a new way of looking at something.

It's interesting to ask yourself where your way of thinking comes from. What way of thinking brought you to where you are now? And how can you overcome your mental roadblocks? The most fundamental programming of our personal operating system is established in our upbringing and early learning experiences during the first seven years of life. During these formative years, we are completely open to absorbing everything as truth, as though we are recorders, observing and storing each experience on our internal hard drive—our subconscious. This process forms the essential foundation of our personal operating system.

From ages 7 to 21, we continue to be profoundly influenced by various external factors, such as the internet, the news, and friends.

From early on, we're confronted with a vast amount of information, advice, and lessons from parents, teachers, and people in our immediate surroundings. All this information has an unimaginable influence on the brain, particularly the young brain.

Individuals who are mainly focused on growth have far less of a need to prove that they've earned their spurs in a certain area. They see challenges as an opportunity to learn new things and failures as a sign that they still have a way to go, which is a path they want to follow because that's how progress gets made. They face their own mistakes and shortcomings honestly and can move forward from a place of trust that's based on facts. Setbacks also then have less of an impact on self-confidence than they do on people who have a static mindset.

If you believe you're capable of developing, you're open to precise information about your current abilities, even if it's not very flattering. And if you're focused on learning, you need that information to be able to do it properly. Those with a static mindset assess information about their abilities as mainly good or bad. They're afraid to fail because they think failure reflects negatively on their basic skills.

Now it's up to you to analyze your own thought patterns. In what situations is your mindset static, and when are you more growth-focused?

> *"Radical change is not a matter*
> *of time or capacity, the ability to change.*
> *It's a matter of intrinsic motivation:*
> *having a desire or a need*
> *and having the will to do it."*

Your Mental Wiring

Your thought processes are the result of conditioning. You have been mentally wired. In this respect, your thinking isn't free. It's the result of your ancestry, your upbringing, your gender, the people around you, your socio-political and economic background, the books you read, your experiences, and the information that's been pumped into you over the years. This means your thinking has been programmed, usually incorrectly, and drenched in biases and divergent opinions.

Here are some examples of what I mean:

> "I'm not worth it."
> "I'm not good enough."
> "It'll never work."
> "I can't."

"Becoming financially free is impossible."
"That's not for our kind of people."
"Men/women are unreliable."
"Money isn't important."
"Everything's expensive."
"Rich and successful people are always
bad and mean."
"The chance of success is close to zero."
"If I quit smoking, I'll gain at least 20 pounds."
"I've tried everything, but those pounds
keep coming back."
"Some people have all the luck—
all the bad stuff happens to me."
"That's how I am. I can't do anything
about it."

These things aren't facts, but beliefs that have come about because of erroneous information that your subconscious has assumed to be true. We link an expectation or a consequence to an action or event. That association is the neural connection that we make from which our conviction arises.

Suppose that as a child, you were once startled by a barking dog, and at that moment your mother shouted out, "Watch out, that dog's dangerous!" Now, when you encounter a dog on the street today, it's quite possible you get scared and your heart starts racing, while I, in the same situation, would pet the animal and start playing with it. Your nervous system made a connection between "dog" and "danger," while my connection is "dog" and "cuddly." The same dog and the same situation but experienced from different perspectives. It's not the situation that determines things, but how you deal with it. That physical response is always the result of the signals your body receives from your brain. In other words, conditioning largely determines your behavior.

Scientific research shows that approximately 5% of your behavior is conscious. These are the choices and actions you consciously think about. The vast majority of it (95%) is driven by your subconscious. Many of the things you do happen on autopilot: talking, moving, blinking your eyes, breathing, eating. When you're driving, you probably sometimes notice that you're suddenly a lot further down the road than you expected. In those moments, driving doesn't have your full attention. Unconsciously, though, you do manage to drive. You can probably find everything blindfolded in the supermarket where you do your weekly grocery shopping. That is, until they change the shelves around. Test your own unconscious behavior by, for example, moving your trash can from the kitchen to another place in the house. Have a go at counting how many times you unconsciously walk to the usual place in the first few days.

"Change takes time," I often hear, or "Changing your behavior or habits doesn't just happen." That's correct. Lasting change is created by repeating a new habit and working on it every day. The change itself, however, is the result of a decision you make in a fraction of a second. My father stopped smoking cold turkey after 40 years. It happened the day he was whisked off, sirens blaring, to the hospital. He'd had a heart attack, and a few hours later, he had a quintuple bypass. He still sometimes longs for a cigarette, but he's never lit one up again.

Radical change is not a matter of time or capacity, the ability to change. It's a matter of intrinsic motivation: having a desire or need and having the will to do it.

If there's no immediate need present, a new pattern of behavior usually takes time to set in. A different way of thinking or a new lifestyle is first created by building a very small, new neural pathway. Think of that forest again, where you work to carve out a new path through all those trees and bushes. That path has to be hewn through a jungle of obstacles that quickly reclaim it. "Just come on back to the five-lane highway," your more established behavior calls out. It's so easy to fall back into. But when the path becomes passable and you keep using it regularly, it becomes more and more ingrained until it, too, is laid well enough to quickly carry along your new behavior. This process requires awareness, attention, and discipline.

To create lasting change, you first need to know that you can change anything at any time. And once again, the decision to change takes no time. Not changing it and just mulling it over it does. The greater the need or your desire, the less discipline, willpower, and perseverance you need. Know that you and you alone are responsible for yourself and your behavior. Take responsibility—whatever the circumstances may be. Only then do you have control over yourself or, in management terms, do you have personal leadership. Live your life based on your own rules, the ones you have put down in your personal statute.

"Your daily existence is a reflection of your thoughts."

Reprogram Your Personal Operating System

Your daily life is a reflection of your thoughts, so you should shift your attention to what you want. Be sure your state of being is positive. And be as concrete as possible: for example, "I want to net $100,000 a year" instead of "I want to earn enough money" or "I don't want any more financial worries."

Not "I don't want to be unhappy anymore," but "I want to be happy" or better still, "I feel happy." Don't fall into vagaries such as "I want to have cool, nice friends around me," "I'd like to have more time for myself," "I just want a nice life," or "When there's time, I'm going to do what I really like." These are intentions and they'll give you direction, but they're like shooting blanks.

First you must determine what you really want and what's holding you back now. Let's go back to the fundamental questions. Where do you want to go? Where are you now? And what's keeping you from achieving that goal right now? Do you lack something? Is there a limiting belief? Is someone standing in your way? Is it your energy level? Is it certain emotions? If you're angry, disappointed, down, or irritated, you'll generally tend to focus on what you don't want instead of what you do. "I don't want to be sad." "I don't want to be lonely." "I don't want to be fat." "I don't want to feel so crappy." I don't want this; I don't want that. If you stay focused on what you don't want, your head will be filled with those thoughts, and you'll be endlessly preoccupied by them.

It's often the influences of parents or events from our younger years that are deeply ingrained in our operating system. Because I've coached many people personally and professionally in recent years, it's become clear to me that the personal operating system is all too often programmed to never get you where you want to go. This is either because that destination isn't clear, or because the system keeps rerouting us. If you don't notice that, it'll keep you roaming around aimlessly for years.

You can break through that pattern by analyzing your self-image. Why do you do what you do, and what's that based on? Next, decide what you want. That has to be so crystal clear that you can easily outline it.

Describe what happiness entails for you. What needs to happen to make you feel happy? Take time to think about this— it's extremely important. Ask yourself concrete and specific questions. How much time do you want for yourself, and what do you need that time for? Only when you determine how you're going to spend that time will your subconscious start to cooperate to meet your wishes.

It works the same with money as it does with time; you only get motivated to save money when you know what you want to spend that money on. That can be a pair of shoes you're in love with, a new car, a property, or a vacation. It can even be achieving financial independence. My question then is: What do you mean by that? How much money do you need to be financially independent? Or do you mean that you have a basic monthly amount at your disposal so you can lead a carefree existence? Make that amount concrete.

And make sure you know what the "why" is. The reason you want something—or even better, why you long for it—determines how powerful your intrinsic motivation is. In all instances, write down the amount you need. Let it penetrate into your subconscious. To achieve this, your rational mind has to be willing to entertain positive feelings, a powerful emotion. But first, ensure that you have absolute clarity. Ask yourself specific, clear questions and make what you want concrete by writing down your questions and answers.

Clarity is essential to achieving your goals. Next, you have to find out what's keeping you from achieving what you want so you can systematically overcome those obstacles.

Ask yourself what the benefits of will be breaking through your negative behavior and changing it into positive behavior. It doesn't all need to work out on the first try, but you need to take immediate action and make progress. You need a weighty incentive to get results. You have to create extra pain and pleasure for yourself; otherwise your intention will be noncommittal. Turn your "want to" into a "must!" You "have to" for yourself, not for anyone else. You get to determine the rules, but if you want to be successful, if you want to live your best life, you'll have to stick to those rules. Discipline is about making agreements with yourself and sticking to them. Necessity and desire are our primary driving forces. If your desire isn't strong enough, then you don't really want it. You say you want something, but you don't do much about it. Apparently, there's not enough of a necessity. You don't really want it. There's not enough need, and you don't have enough self-discipline.

Don't you think that's odd? You know that a better life is possible, but you accept your less desirable situation, and you get what you accept. You tell yourself that things are fine the way they are to obscure the fact that you've failed. Because you're afraid of failing. Your longing for "sustainable" pleasure loses out to the fear of sacrifice. And that's why you don't act—because then there's no risk of failure.

Ask yourself: "What will happen to me and my life if I don't change this behavior, this habit?" And then think of one thing you can do today—but aren't doing yet—that will have a significant positive impact on your quality of life, especially if it's a part of your daily life. Something you can do right away but have kept putting off.

Ed asked himself that question. He'd come to a master class with his wife. At the end of the day, he came up to me. His lip was quivering, his eyes red. He stretched out his arm and pressed a packet of cigarettes into my hand. "I quit!" he shouted. "I'm done!" He looked me right in the eye and held his gaze for seconds. Big tears were running down his cheeks. I felt his powerlessness.

A few weeks later, I received an email from him in which he shared his experiences: "I came along that weekend with the nonchalant, negative mindset of 'We'll see.' But I was immediately touched and became calm, something I hadn't experienced in years. The second day, during your story about your own bad lifestyle, I could only think 'That's how I live. What am I doing to my wife and myself?' I'd often thought I needed to stop smoking, but your story and what you said—'Just fucking do it'—were so convincing. Like a knife cutting through me. After thirty years of smoking shag, I immediately decided to quit that afternoon. What did I have to lose? My own life. I also started eating and drinking healthier. It's been good for our relationship, I dare to show the real me more, and I'm really enjoying life again!"

Ed has never smoked again, he left his job and started working as an independent contractor in electrical engineering, and he has more work than he can take on. That one afternoon, he made two important decisions that gave shape to his best life.

Assignment

Think about one thing you want to change about yourself, your behavior, or your current situation. Make the decision now that you really want it and that you're going to change it. Think of every kind of pain you can, so you can associate your old behavior and the adverse consequences it has or will have on your life and your happiness if you don't change it. Imagine the worst possible outcome. Then think about the pleasant feelings you can associate with what you're going to change. Is this change a "have to" for you? So, then, what are you going to do?

Be honest—no fooling yourself allowed here. It's the only way to generate the critical insights you need. You'll get a rough idea of who you are, deep inside, and you'll sketch a picture of your best life. Hold that image in your mind. Take time for it.

Intention: Write down what you'd like to change about yourself and your life. Are you struggling with certain feelings? Would you like to change something about your behavior? What are your wishes? What dreams do you want to make come true?

Motivation: Next, write down why you want to change the things you mentioned above, or why you think you should change them. Explain why you want to fulfill your dreams.

Sabotage: If you know what you want to change and you're motivated to do so, why haven't you done it yet? If you have a dream to fulfill, what's the reason you haven't done so yet?

Sacrifice: There's no success without sacrifice. If you want to reach your goals and make your dreams come true, you'll have to do something for it and give something up. The bigger the goals and dreams, the bigger the sacrifices you'll be making. You'll have to work hard for them. You'll have to spend time on things, which will eat into your social life and fun times. What are you willing to give up to make your dreams come true?

Positive consequences: What will happen and how will you feel if you change that part of yourself and your life changes as a result? What can or will the positive consequences be if you accomplish this?

Negative consequences: What will happen if you don't take action yet again? What will happen with your life if you don't change anything now? How will you feel in a month, a year, or five years from now if you don't start living up to your intentions? What can be or will be the negative consequences for you and the rest of your life if you don't take steps right away? Describe the worst-case scenario. How does that feel?

Let me repeat this. This assignment only works if you write down the answers. Think about what you want to change about yourself and your life. Imagine how you'll feel when you have the life you want. What will the positive consequences be? Also imagine what'll happen if everything stays the same. You'll have only yourself to blame if you don't take full advantage of the opportunity you've been given.

> *"If you think you are beaten, you are;*
> *If you think you dare not, you don't.*
> *If you'd like to win, but you think you can't,*
> *It is almost certain you won't.*
> *If you think you'll lose, you've lost; For out*
> *in this world we find Success begins with a*
> *fellow's will It's all in the state of mind.*
> *If you think you're outclassed, you are;*
> *You've got to think high to rise.*
> *You've got to be sure of yourself before*
> *You can ever win the prize.*

Life's battles don't always go
To the stronger or faster man;
But sooner or later the man who wins
Is the one who thinks he can!"

— **Walter D. Wintle, from**
Think and Grow Rich

Limiting Beliefs

You want to enjoy yourself, give meaning to your existence, be there for people you care about, learn, and grow. What's holding you back? It's almost always limiting thought patterns that keep us from achieving what we want. They're false beliefs that delude us.

Limiting thought patterns are like invisible bars. They hold you captive and make it impossible to grow or move forward in life. Those thought patterns have formed into a road map, the map in your personal navigation system. You can probably imagine that any journey is going to be a difficult one if your map is incorrect and full of dead ends. And it really gets problematic if that map can never get you where you want to go because the desired destinations aren't on it. Suppose you want to go to Barcelona or Bali, but your personal map stops at your country's borders. Those destinations you want to go to simply don't exist in your system. Then how are you ever going to get there?

It works the same way with your beliefs and convictions. If you're convinced that something is impossible, that you can't do it, then that's how it will be; therefore, those limiting beliefs set the boundaries of your playing field. That is your reality. It's therefore tremendously important that you uncover all your limiting thoughts, acknowledge them, and then know how to break through them. Only then can you escape from that invisible prison.

Break Through Your Self-Limiting Patterns

Cindy and I experienced this ourselves during the renovation of our country house. We had designed a new layout for all the rooms based on the existing interior walls. However, that layout came with many limitations, and we couldn't make the most practical choices. That was until the contractor tore down all the non-load-bearing walls, creating large open spaces. Suddenly, we were able to think more freely and see new possibilities, which led to a completely different plan and a much better layout for the house.

When you start thinking about your future with the same open mind, suddenly a lot more becomes possible—probably more than you initially thought. It can be overwhelming at first, but it's crucial to think about your future without immediately imposing limits. By doing so, you can discover what you truly want, without letting doubt or constraints hold you back. This gives you direction. Once you've figured that out, you can start exploring what you need to achieve it and how you can make it happen. And when you're clear on that, you can make decisions that will allow your life to develop in the direction you desire.

What mental walls are holding you back? First you have to be aware of your beliefs and patterns to then be able to consciously and purposefully disrupt them. Then you have to recondition yourself with a new positive behavior.

During a question-and-answer session, Elma broke through her self-limiting patterns. She had built a successful cosmetics business but could not manage herself. She overcame her fear and shame by stepping on stage with the massive amount of excess weight she carried. "I felt terrible," she told me a few months later. "I just wanted to disappear, but it was really an eye-opener."

Because it was clear that she was particularly good at running her business, I had suggested in that session that she think of herself as "Elma, Inc." On the spot, a new insight emerged. "Suddenly it was so logical and clear," she said. "I immediately started investing much more time in myself and lost more than 20 pounds in a few weeks. Now I really take time for myself. I also started thinking differently. Before, I always thought 'I don't want to be fat.' Now I think 'I want to be healthy and slim.' Business-wise, I have become more confident and things are going great. My wish was to double our revenue, but during your lessons I really learned to believe in it by writing it down. Meanwhile, our revenue has tripled. We have also moved to a beautiful place abroad, where I have found more peace and can enjoy life. Amazing? Maybe, but I know now that nothing is impossible."

Elma was able to break through her old mindset and replace it with another in a short period of time. Of course, she is highly disciplined, but her motivation is fueled by what she continues to achieve. The results are visible, and results don't lie.

It's important that you get fulfillment from the new associations you use when you're consciously working on changing your behavior. If that isn't the case, you'll build up internal resistance, and it'll take much more effort and energy to get where you want. It's not only about making a rational (intellectual) connection, but especially about making an emotional one—that's what determines whether your new pattern will be a lasting one. Emotion is necessary for programming new associations (connections) in your brain. You want to stop experiencing pain and, instead, feel great because of the change in your behavior. Learning a new pattern or new behavior only works if your new, desired pattern is linked to a concrete plan, self-discipline, a positive outcome, and a reward. Without a plan and without discipline, all you have is an intention, a good resolution.

Limiting Beliefs About Money

For many people, money is a limiting phenomenon. Maybe the words "rich" and "money" also create some level of discomfort within you. What meaning do you assign to money? Do you think it's unimportant? Would you rather have structural money concerns? I doubt it. That's not what you want. Nobody wants to be poor, and nobody wants to worry about money. Everybody wants to be rich, only "being rich" has different connotations for everyone.

By being rich, I don't mean chasing after huge piles of cash. It also has nothing to do with selfishness or greed. I don't know the exact numbers, but we could say that most of the people in the United States are rich. We have roofs over our heads, we can eat what we want every day, we're reasonably free to think what we want, we live in freedom (albeit bound by a lot of laws and regulations), and we have a government with a reasonably good social welfare system. Compared to the living conditions of many other people on this planet, that is wealth.

Money matters in our Western society. Without money, you can't buy groceries or pay the rent or mortgage. Without money, you can't afford a pleasant life. Without money, no vacations. Without money, you can't have fun eating out with friends. Without money, you can't buy gifts for people you want to give things to. Without money, you can't pay for a good education for your children or invest in your own future. And investing in yourself is the best investment you can make. Without adequate financial resources, you can't get good medical care when you need it. Not for your parents, not for your children, and not for yourself.

A young woman who'd already done several master classes and was a successful independent freelancer once sent me a very moving email. In it, she wrote that she was also someone to whom money had never mattered. To her great horror, she'd been diagnosed with breast cancer. The importance of money suddenly became more than clear to her. She'd never taken out good disability insurance because it was too expensive. Because of her health issues, she was unable to work for the time being, and the medical care she acutely needed didn't come cheap.

I'd like to share a passage from that email with you:

"Money and wealth, which you talked about during your master class—I had trouble with that. I know better now. Because since I've been diagnosed with cancer without disability insurance, it's suddenly become very clear to me that money's not a luxury, but a sheer necessity."

Money regularly seems to lead to the limiting thought pattern: I don't need to get rich. It doesn't matter what exactly you mean by this—being a millionaire or having enough money to live comfortably and carefree—but with this thought, you send a signal to your subconscious. What your subconscious hears is: keep money at bay. Then your operating system goes out of its way to fulfill this "wish" because that's the energy you're putting out there.

It's important to first recognize any limiting thoughts you have. It isn't easy to uncover your own limiting thoughts, because you don't know what you don't know. That means you need guidance to gain those insights. This book can help you, as can a coach, who can serve as a mirror for you.

Suppose your limiting thought is "I don't need to become rich." If you recognize that thought, the next step is to find out what negative associations you have toward money. These could be thoughts like "To make money you have to work extremely hard," "Rich people are mean and selfish," or "Money is the root of all evil in the world."

When you have the belief that money and happiness don't go together, you build up resistance to any thoughts related to money. The association with money is then negative and can even generate a form of pain. After all, for you, money then means you cannot be happy, and you want to keep money from making you unhappy. From that point on, this is the map that's programmed into your personal navigation system. Your subconscious will do everything it can to keep money at bay. It'll steer you in another direction; it will try to steer you away from opportunities and situations that could generate money. Or rather, instead of attracting money, you'll both consciously and unconsciously repel it.

A limiting thought could be that your environment determines success and wealth. Your environment certainly matters, but if that were a universal truth, everyone in one town would be rich, and everyone in another would be poor. That's not the case. Every big and small town has wealthier people and less wealthy people. Are you convinced that education and level of knowledge are decisive factors in success and wealth? Because there are college-educated people who live average lives, and there are people with tremendous financial wealth who have had little formal education. Once again, your environment has a huge impact on you, but ultimately the determining factor is how you deal with it. It's about your mindset and the choices you make.

You can discover for yourself what your limiting beliefs are, by asking questions. Once it's clear what your limiting thoughts are and what incorrect associations are in your system, you can overwrite that by programming new information, information that is accurate, for example: Money is a means by which I can improve the quality of my existence. By having adequate financial resources, I have no money worries, no stress, I can go out to eat with friends, travel with my partner and children, take better care of my family, buy what I'd like, and I am able to be there for others financially. You can do a lot of good things with money, and you can always give it away. There are plenty of people and creatures in need.

Create a Positive Money Mindset

Here's another way of looking at money: it's a means of exchange. By buying something or paying for a service, you offer someone a job, enabling them to earn a living. And when they spend part of their money, others are helped in the same way. In principle, that's a sound economic model. And in a healthy economy, money has to keep moving. The circulation of money works like oxygen to the economy. When less money is spent, the financial system suffocates.

I'll give you a simple example. Thank you for buying this book. In doing so, you've given money to the tax authorities, the mail carrier, the people at the logistics center, the printer, the paper supplier, the copyeditor, the editor, the designer, the publisher, and me, the writer. The investment you've made contributes to the livelihoods of many people. And now it's up to you to discover the tremendous added value of this book. Then you'll see how big the return you can make on this investment is. If you do what I teach you in this book, it can net you a lot of value and money.

Free yourself from your limiting beliefs about money. Repeating positive thoughts (affirmations) about money day in, day out creates new neural associations, new connections in your brain. If you have a not-so-positive view of money, you can change that belief. And if your views are positive, having a positive, conscious view of money can only strengthen your beliefs.

Finally, some valuable advice: don't only look at what something costs, but also at the return on your investment. For each expense or each investment you make, ask yourself these four questions:

1. What does it cost?
2. What will it bring me?
   (This doesn't only have to be measured in money.)
3. Can I afford it?
   (Or: What can I do to raise the required amount?)
4. What do I think it's worth?
   (Do I have that kind of money?)

"Fear is a state of mind and a feeling you create yourself."

Fear Is Just a Thought

What I'm about to share now is incredibly important. I encourage you to read this section extra carefully. While reading, stop every now and then to ask yourself how much influence fear has on you.

Most of the time, what really stops you from doing what you would like to do is fear. And fear is also a thought—a destructive one, but it is still a thought. Fear has a direct influence on the quality of your life. Fear can paralyze you both mentally and physically. Fear is almost always the result of your imagination. It's visualizing what you are afraid of, what you don't want to happen.

It's a state of mind and a feeling you create yourself. When you allow those fears and emotions in and enter into dialogue with them in your thoughts, they seem to become reality. And as long as fearful thoughts are swirling around in your mind, your subjective reality will be confirmed, and success will hide out until the coast is clear.

You're afraid of thoughts you can't control. And when you can't control your thoughts, it means your thoughts have power over you. That powerless feeling devours energy and makes you insecure and unhappy. Fearful thoughts can be so destructive that they can destroy any chance of success and, ultimately, a human life.

A lack of self-esteem, self-insight, and clarity leads to restlessness, doubt, mood swings, fear, and dissatisfaction. Letting your mind wander into the future or the past robs you of strength in the here and now. Looking back is dangerous if you want to move forward, but at certain moments when your life is difficult, you sometimes need to look back; self-reflection is necessary. It's then you see that all the baggage from your past and the anchors you've thrown out over the years—your self-limiting thought patterns—have chained you in place. A ship at anchor cannot set sail. To feel free and be unencumbered, you have to cast off those chains.

And before you can cast them off, you first have to find them. What anchors are weighing you down? Fear and uncertainty often arise from chaotic thoughts, a lack of clarity. It's almost impossible to eliminate fear from our minds, but you can learn to detect it early and deal with it consciously.

The essential question here is: What are you afraid of? Do you have a clear answer for this? How can you be afraid of something if you can't clearly explain what it is? Study your fear. What are you, in fact, afraid of? Ask yourself that question and really think about it. Once an answer comes to mind, dig deeper. Don't be vague and general; specifically name what you're afraid of. Why are you afraid of this potential outcome? What's your biggest fear?

If you continue to ask questions until you no longer can, you'll discover the real underlying issue that your fear is based on. Then you can study the source of that fear. It's also good to think about the worst thing that could possibly happen, and then ask yourself how realistic that horrific outcome is. That way, you can also figure out what you can do to prevent it from happening. And finally, you can imagine what you'd be capable of if this fear no longer had a hold on you.

Some well-known primary fears are fear of failure, fear of criticism, fear of poverty, fear of loss of a loved one, fear of becoming ill, fear of old age, and fear of death.

The primary fears that commonly arise are

1. The fear that you are not enough
2. The fear of judgment and others' opinions
3. The fear that no one loves you

We deeply long for appreciation and recognition; these are basic, universal needs that every human being has. For many people, these are even important personal values. If you feel you're not appreciated, you'll soon feel unhappy. The criticism of others, rightly or wrongly, affects you and can make you insecure. How is that possible? Maybe you lack self-esteem and self-confidence, or perhaps the judgment of others feels unjust.

Yet it can go even further than that. The opinions of others can present serious obstacles. Even though they may have nothing to do with the actual situation, your emotions can be strongly influenced by them. At times like those, you completely drown in a fictional world of thought that creates your own reality. Your fear and uncertainty flow from assumptions that aren't based on facts or actual events. You allow yourself to believe in myths, and that's not without consequences. Again, you see here: you become what you think.

Fear of failure is an extremely common basic fear. When I hear that people are afraid of failure, I ask what they mean by "failure." "That things will go wrong." "That things won't go as I'd planned." Personally, I've found that almost nothing goes the way you think it will. For this reason, you always have to be flexible and prepared to make decisions and perhaps adjustments—as long as you reach your final goal. And even that's not always possible. You might then think things went wrong, but did they fail completely? Are you a failure? Have you failed? What you did may have produced a different result than you originally had in mind, but the trick is to then change something in your approach and continue to do so until you have reached the desired goal.

Learn from every action you take. Learn from every setback. Learn from every situation and every problem. Only when something is entirely unsuccessful and you learn nothing from it can you say that your initiative was pointless. In that case, you may perhaps speak of failure.

Once more the question: What is failure? What are you afraid of? Who decides whether you've messed up, failed, or succeeded? You or the outside world? Again, you're not in control of yourself when you give other people—the outside world—the power to judge whether you're doing something right or not. Why would you allow that? Why should you care what others think? Because you want their approval and appreciation?

As long as you're afraid of failure, you won't be ready for success. As long as you're controlled by your fears, you'll never become change-minded and never feel free and happy. There are people who sit in traffic jams every day, don't get satisfaction from their work, and think they're underpaid, but over the years they've grown accustomed. It feels safe. They're comfortably unhappy. They complain about things, but they also feel safe in that situation. Changing their lives in favor of a better future is scary. That's why they do nothing. It's better to be unhappy in uncomfortable security than to take a chance at success and happiness.

When you're having self-limiting thoughts or fears, ask yourself the question: "Is this true?" Byron Katie asks four questions in her worldwide bestseller *The Work*:

"Is it true?"

"Can you absolutely know that it's true?"

"How do you react, what happens, when you believe that thought?"

"Who would you be without that thought?"

Once again, you see that the power of asking targeted questions leads to insight. Good questions are a mirror and show you not only what you want, but above all, what you need.

"I've had a lot of worries in my life,
most of which never happened."

– Mark Twain

You Are the Problem

People tend to believe that it's their problems that create obstacles rather than their own thinking. When a problem arises, they often think it's because of someone else. Their partner or ex, parents, children, colleagues, friends, or someone who just bothers them. The problem also could be not knowing the right people or having too little money, or too little time. There are all sorts of problems we may face, but much of the time, they're created in the mind.

How many nights have you lain awake in bed dwelling on the most dramatic scenarios that have never come to pass? Most of the worries that preoccupy us are conjured up in our imaginations. The scenarios you fret over usually seem different the next day and often take a much less dramatic turn. If you remain stuck in worry or fixated on "a problem," you feed the negative.

In the first session I had with my Buddhist teacher Tulku Lobsang, he literally said, "You are the problem." Without you, the problem wouldn't exist, because it exists in your mind. It's about what you think about something and how you deal with it. You can also see that problem as an issue for which you don't yet have a solution.

According to Buddhist philosophy, problems are there to teach us. They come on your path to teach you something and frequently have to do with your life themes, the lessons you need to learn at certain points in your life. If you don't sort out the right way to deal with a problem or find a solution, that problem will keep showing up in different guises on your life path. Only when you've shown that you've understood the lesson can you proceed to the next level, just like in a game. And once you're there, you'll encounter new obstacles to overcome. So don't hope for things to get easier, but make sure you keep working on yourself. Don't hope for fewer challenges, but make sure you have more skills to deal with them. Don't hope for fewer problems, but make sure you have more insights and wisdom. Don't wish it was easier. Wish you were better.

Taking Stock of Your Life

For years, I interviewed hundreds of people by means of a test on self-knowledge, awareness, and insight. One of the questions was "What do you think will make you happier?" An additional assignment was to describe what they would like their daily lives to be like.

"I'd like to be more in balance," was one of the most common answers, but almost no one could concretely explain what they meant by that. As a result, that led to new questions. "How do I create more balance so I'm happier in life?" "What can I do to achieve a better balance between my work, my family, my friends, and myself?"

Balance is created when you clearly know what you want and are conscious of what you're doing. After that, the key is to chart your own course and not be distracted by all the opinions and judgments that come your way.

In a conversation with Ann, she told me she'd become somewhat out of balance because of the good opinions of people around her. During our conversation, what mainly became clear to me was that she was lacking structure and an overview of what was going on. As a result, she'd become overwhelmed by a restless feeling, and adrenaline and cortisol were pumping through her body. She was stressed, carrying tension in her lower abdomen, and breathing irregularly.

"What do you mean by 'I want to be in balance'?" I asked Ann. She looked out across the room, where 1500 pairs of eyes were fixed on her. "Well, I just do," she mumbled. And then, slightly irritated,

"You should know what I mean."

"I think I know," I said, "but it's about what you mean by it."

Ann sighed. "I think it's a sign of weakness, and that's just not at all who I am." This powerful woman was running a company and the mother of two young children. What meaning was Ann assigning to her thoughts? "You know," she said, staring off a little dreamily, "Sometimes I just have had enough of defending to everyone the fact that I'm successful, that we're taking another vacation, that I have another new outfit, that I really don't neglect my children, and that I'm lucky to have my figure. As if it's all a given."

I smiled. "That's a relief, isn't it?" I said that peace and balance are mainly related to mindset: whether she had control over her thoughts, or whether they had control over her. "Don't worry about what others think of you, because that's what's knocking you off balance."

You can only be in balance if you're the center of your own life. Think of your life as a circle. To feel balanced, you have to be right in the middle of that circle. Life takes place around you. That isn't selfish; it's the right positioning to maintain an overview and divide your time evenly between your family, your work, your friends, and yourself. If you make yourself unimportant, you'll be offside and feel the imbalance immediately.

I explained this to Ann during the master class. In her superwoman role, she was in the spotlight, both at her own company and in her family. As a result of the criticism of others, however, she'd increasingly moved into the background. Ann performed best as a striker, but she increasingly found herself playing defense, and in that position she felt uncomfortable.

From the many conversations I've had, it's become clear to me that for most people, the desire to be more in balance means that their current lifestyle is out of balance. They don't have a clear overview of what they're doing, they have no control over their own schedule, and their troubling thoughts make them feel uncertain. The way forward here is to create structure. To foster clarity and create an overview: in other words, awareness. Awareness brings insight. It generates more self-confidence and tranquility, especially in one's mind.

I asked Ann to give me her planner. "You think you have to do way too much in too little time, that you have to arrange everything for everyone," I said to her. "And you worry about what others think of you. That originates in your thoughts. That's your self-image, and that self-image is nothing more than a thought. But because you've carried that thought around with you for so long, you've begun to act in accordance with it. And now it's your reality. Change your thoughts, and your life will change." In the meantime, I was crossing out a number of (in my opinion) less important things in her schedule and adding an hour of Ann-time three times a week. "Make agreements with yourself and stick to them."

"Yes, but ..." she interrupted me bossily as I was giving her calendar back. I gave her a stern smile and made a gesture of gratitude with my hands.

Act As If Nothing and No One Bothers You

Think about a time when someone's words hurt you. Maybe it was a cutting remark from a colleague or harsh criticism from a stranger. How did it make you feel? Angry? Hurt? Sad? Defeated? What if you could let those words roll off your back, rendering them powerless? That's the art of acting as if nothing and no one bothers you. It's about mastering your mind and deciding that external negativity won't affect your internal peace.

Years ago, I was a young entrepreneur with big dreams. But there were two moments that deeply affected me. Leaving Radio 538 involved several legal battles, and my first major business deal didn't go as expected. During that time, I felt emotionally unbalanced and, above all, powerless. Until I realized that by feeling this way, I was giving my power to others who determined how I felt. From that moment on, I decided that nothing and no one would be able to affect me anymore—not by ignoring the world around me, but by building a mindset so strong that external factors could no longer shake me.

If something affects you, it's because you've allowed it to. Something touches you because it holds meaning for you. It doesn't mean you need to become completely numb. But it is a sign that your self-esteem and confidence are not strong enough to protect you.

Most opinions, judgments, and criticisms from others have very little to do with you. People project their own fears, insecurities, or envy. Once you understand this, others' opinions will affect you less. The only opinion that truly matters is your own. And even then, you must be both your toughest critic and your greatest supporter.

I'm not saying you should ignore all feedback. Constructive criticism can be valuable. But there is a big difference between constructive feedback and useless criticism. Seek feedback from people whose opinions you trust and value.

As you start to care less about what others think of you, something remarkable happens. The things that used to affect you won't have the same impact anymore. And as you are less influenced by negativity, you'll find that you have more positive energy for yourself.

Think about how much time and energy you waste worrying about what others think of you. And you know it—what you think others think of you is really just what you think of yourself.

Changing your mindset is not easy. It's like building a muscle. It takes time, effort, and repeated practice. A simple technique I use is to ask questions. Why does this person's opinion matter? Why does this comment affect me? Why is this bothering me so much? Usually, what affects you is the meaning you assign to what someone else has said or done. By consciously analyzing this way, you can respond more rationally rather than emotionally.

Make a commitment to live by your own rules. Don't be swayed by others, and don't give anyone the power to affect you emotionally. When you do this, you will discover an inner peace, freedom, and strength that will transform your life.

> *"My life is filled with blessings,*
> *and for that, I am grateful."*

A Gratitude Mindset

Inner peace allows you to perceive the world around you differently. Feelings of gratitude will arise sooner. Say "thank you" more often, even if you do it silently. Two little words with tremendous weight. Be grateful for what you have rather than unhappy about what you don't have. Gratitude generates feelings of enlightenment and happiness. You can increase your state of consciousness and your energy level by showing gratitude, not out of courtesy, but out of humility and admiration. You make yourself bigger by making yourself small. Being sincerely grateful is a token of appreciation and an expression of kindness.

You can practice gratitude every day. To help you do that, I've included some guided meditations about gratitude in the Meditation Moments app. For example, before you go to sleep, take 10 minutes of quiet time for yourself. Close your eyes and calmly breathe in and out a few times. Feel what happens in your body. Then ask yourself: "What am I grateful for today?" Ask that question from your heart. "What am I grateful for today? I'm grateful for this beautiful day, for every new opportunity, for the life that flows through me, for the people who care about me, for the wonderous nature on this planet, for the sun that rises for us every day and never asks for anything in return. My life is filled with blessings, and for that, I am grateful." Do this every night when you go to bed. Every day there are things to be grateful for, and rounding off your day with appreciative thoughts has a positive influence on your subconscious. When you do that on a daily basis, you'll discover that you go to sleep feeling good. Be grateful, and you'll feel happier.

Gratitude also allows you to connect with Cosmic Intelligence. I mentioned it earlier, and Wallace D. Wattles didn't devote an entire chapter to gratitude in *The Science of Getting Rich* for no reason. Wattles' conviction is that a mindset of sincere gratitude connects you energetically with the mystical power of the uni verse. Gratitude puts goodness and happiness on your life path. How does it work? It has to do with the wonderful cosmic law of attraction and creation.

> *"If you spend your time*
> *chasing butterflies,*
> *they'll fly away.*
> *But if you spend time*
> *creating a beautiful garden,*
> *the butterflies will come.*
> *Don't chase, attract what you*
> *wish for."*

The Law of Attraction and Creation

Becoming successful is the result of both thinking and doing. True success comes when you understand how cosmic forces can work for you. There are natural laws in the universe, like gravity and electricity, but they don't explain everything.

The greatest teachers, sages, and scientists have all recognized that there are universal forces influencing everything. One key law to understand is the law of attraction and creation. Everything is made of energy fields, and this energy vibrates at specific frequencies.

"Nothing happens until something moves," said Albert Einstein. Everything in the universe moves and evolves, including you. Your body's cells constantly change. Each person's unique energy is made up of frequencies from both body and mind, and even thoughts have measurable frequencies.

Energy is tangible—you can feel comfortable around some people and uneasy around others because of their energy field. According to the law of attraction, similar energies attract each other. If you feel a deep connection with someone, you're on the same wavelength. When strong emotions mix with thoughts and belief, they create a frequency that your subconscious picks up and emits, like a radio station sending a signal. These vibrations, which can be scientifically measured, are sent to Cosmic Intelligence, where the mystery of attraction and creation begins.

This law originated with the creation of everything. It has always been and will always be. It is the basis of existence, of everything that is. The entire structure of the universe is determined by cosmic laws. The position of the sun and moon and all the stars can be calculated years out with great precision. These same cosmic laws also govern our lives. The law of attraction and creation is the process of energetic transformation, the creation and transformation of energy into tangible matter. A thought is energy. Whether you believe it or not, you are the one who determines how the laws influence your life. How? Through your thoughts.

It's all very complex to understand, and maybe we never will fully grasp it. But I'd like to share my vision on this divine creating force. A simple way to envision the law of attraction is to see yourself as a magnet. We live in the gigantic magnetic field that surrounds the earth. The stronger and more powerful our thoughts are, the more, and the more easily, we can attract things into our lives as we want them. For some people, this happens automatically without them being aware of it. For them, everything always seems to come naturally. They achieve everything they want, accomplish success after success, and are often rewarded with wealth. Others very consciously work on it while accomplishing one great thing after the other. In the first 20 years of my life, I unconsciously applied the law, and then I started to do it more consciously. Successfully, every time.

Tune in to the frequency of the reality you want, and that's what you'll get. This sounds vaguer than it actually is. You do this using visualization. Imagine very visually what you want. And not only see it but feel it. For example, a place where you want to live, the home of your dreams, a sports achievement, an amount you want to earn, a company you want to start, an event you want to plan, a book you want to write, and even your best life. Make the image as concrete and as vivid as possible. Incorporate an intense, pure emotion into that image and feeling—feel the longing for it in your heart and in every cell of your body. See yourself living in the final phase, at the point when you've already reached your goal. Experience how it feels when you are where you want to be. It's then that you're in harmony with the energetic frequency of your goal, and "coincidence," or Cosmic Intelligence, will help you actually reach it.

> *"Our inner world creates the outer world.*
> *Our vibrations, the patterns of our thoughts,*
> *attitudes, and actions, are what creates*
> *our reality."*

As You Sow, so Shall You Reap

As soon as you draw your attention—your thoughts—to something, those thoughts are fed by more similar thoughts. If your thinking is focused on what you don't want, that's the energy you'll attract, even though you're thinking "This isn't what I want!" That's why negative thoughts are so dangerous. Thoughts are electromagnetic and have frequencies. When you think, those frequencies are emitted and magnetically attract similar things from the same frequency. That's why people sometimes get what they don't want. Their dominant thoughts are more focused on what they don't want than on what they do. Or they don't know what they want; that's also the case for a lot of people.

The law of attraction and creation is a cosmic law. It doesn't judge and condemn; it sees no good or evil. The law gives you what your mind is most preoccupied with. It's about directing your entire consciousness—and therefore, indirectly, your subconscious as well—toward a thought. You have to concentrate completely on that thought. Focus on the positive, not on the negative. If you think: "I don't want … (whatever)," that message is received as a request to bring you something—that you don't want.

It's called a law, but in fact, the law of attraction and creation is the energy that's always present in everyone's life and at all times. It's the energy that connects the dimensions of time and space. When you become aware of this energy, you can tap into the unimaginable power that I call Cosmic Intelligence. With this universal energy from which everything originates, you can create your own reality.

The universe works like a web shop. Place your order—a thought you're convinced of—and that's what you'll receive. This sounds a little simpler than it really is because you also have to take action yourself. Only action leads to results, but it starts with your thoughts and the vibrations those thoughts emit.

When you "order" something in your mind, you have to be specific. Suppose you order pants from an online store. Your order is not "a pair of pants." You must choose the color you want, the style, and the right size. Then you fill out your personal details and pay, and within a few days, your order arrives. The law of attraction and creation works in exactly the same way.

So be sure that your order is crystal clear. Then there are two more conditions. The first one is that your desire must be pure and sincere because the law responds to energy, the vibrational frequencies you broadcast. You have to live and breathe it; it has to flow through your veins and penetrate every cell of your body. The second condition is that you'll be asked what you're willing to sacrifice, what you're willing to do for it, and what you're willing to let go of. There always is a price to pay. Life will give you almost everything you desire, but you must be willing to pay the price. Just like you have to check out in a store if you want to take something with you. Only life asks you to pay in advance. And it's very likely that your dreams and wishes can come true.

As you sow, so shall you reap. See your thoughts as tiny seeds. From the tiniest of seeds, a tree, shrub, or plant will spring up if you care for it properly. The seed of an oak tree has the potential to grow into a mighty oak tree, but it won't happen if you plant that seed in an itty-bitty pot without light and water. That's how it works with our thoughts. Only if we create the right conditions can our thoughts lead to growth and greatness.

The law of attraction teaches us that like attracts like. The energy you put out into the world will attract similar energy back to you. If you act with confidence, you attract more confidence-building opportunities. If you act like a winner, you attract winning circumstances. But it's important to understand that this isn't passive. You don't just sit and wait for success to come to you—you meet it halfway with action. By acting like you're already winning, you accelerate the process.

Here's where the concept of reaping really takes shape. Your consistent actions—your visualization, your belief, your decision to embody the winner you want to be—begin to yield results. Small wins lead to bigger wins, and before you know it, you're standing in the reality you once envisioned. But it all starts with acting like you're already there.

So, how does this apply to your life right now? You may not have hit your ultimate goal yet, but start thinking: How would the version of you who has already succeeded show up today? How would they handle challenges? How would they interact with others? How would they plan their day? When you live in alignment with your future success, you create a powerful force that pulls that future into your present.

Imagine that you've already achieved everything you've ever dreamed of—financial freedom, personal fulfillment, and professional success. Close your eyes and feel it. Breathe in the satisfaction of victory. What if I told you this feeling, this state of being, is the key to actually achieving those dreams? You might be thinking, "But I'm not there yet." And that's where many of us get stuck—waiting to feel like winners before we act like them.

But here's the truth: waiting until you "make it" to act like you've made it is backward. The most successful people didn't wait for external validation before they carried themselves with confidence. They didn't become winners first and then act like it—they acted like winners *before* the world recognized them as such. And that's what you need to do.

The seeds you plant today can grow into the success you'll harvest in the future. So step into your future self. Act and carry yourself as if you're already winning, and watch how the universe aligns with your vision.

> *"Every reward was the result*
> *of hard work, a lot of sacrifices,*
> *perseverance,*
> *and unwavering self-confidence.*
> *I had to endure humiliation,*
> *I was laughed at,*
> *and along the way, I lost.*
> *But I never gave up."*

Act As If You Are Living Your Best Life

What's stopping you from living your absolute best life right now? Take a moment to think about it. What are the excuses swirling in your head? "I'm not good enough." "I don't have the resources."

"It's not the right time." But let me tell you something—that voice inside your head? It's lying.

The real reason you're not living your best life has nothing to do with resources, timing, or being ready. It's because you're not acting as if you are. You're waiting for some perfect moment when all the pieces magically fall into place. But here's the truth: that moment doesn't exist. The time to act is now. The person standing between you and greatness is you. Your mindset is the key.

Think about it—how would you behave if you were already living your dream life? Would you hesitate to seize opportunities? Would fear hold you back from taking bold actions? Of course not. You'd be confident. You'd make decisions with clarity and purpose. So, why aren't you acting like that right now?

Here's why: you're too comfortable. And comfort is the enemy of progress. It's the slow poison that kills your dreams one day at a time. While you sit waiting for success to land in your lap, the world moves on without you. Success doesn't come to those who wait—it comes to those who take action. But here's the twist: you don't have to wait until you've made it to start acting like you have. In fact, that's exactly backward. You need to start acting like you've already made it—right now—if you want to make it a reality.

This isn't about "faking it until you make it." It's about shifting your mindset, embodying the version of yourself that is already successful. When you act as if you've already achieved your goals, your brain starts to believe it. And when your brain believes it, it finds ways to make it true. It's like turning your imagination into a blueprint that your subconscious follows.

So, let me ask you again: What would you do differently if you were already living your best life? How would you speak? How would you carry yourself? How would you face challenges? More importantly, what's stopping you from doing all of that right now—this very moment? Not tomorrow, not when you feel "ready," because here's another truth—you'll never feel fully ready. The most successful people in the world don't wait for readiness; they jump in headfirst and figure it out as they go.

Success isn't about having all the answers in advance. It's about having the guts to ask the right questions, the determination to search for those answers, and the courage to act despite fear. It's about taking massive action, especially when you're scared. Because here's the thing—if you wait for the perfect time, it will never come. Success rewards those who take the leap and adjust along the way.

Make a decision right now. Will you keep living in mediocrity, making excuses, and waiting for the stars to align? Or will you step up and act like the successful person you aspire to be—today? The choice is yours. But remember this: only one of those choices leads to greatness. And you didn't come this far just to be average, did you?

Let's dive into how you can shift your mindset and start acting as if you're already living your best life. Because once you truly master this mindset, there's no limit to what you can achieve.

Your mind is the most powerful tool you have. It's the engine driving your success, the architect of your reality, and the key to unlocking your full potential. Yet most people never learn how to harness its power. They let their minds run on autopilot, controlled by fear, doubt, and limiting beliefs—and then wonder why they aren't living the life they want.

Here's the reality: mindset isn't some vague, fluffy concept—it's the foundation of everything. Everything you do, everything you achieve, everything you become stems from your mindset. When you master your mindset, you master your life.

So how do you develop a mindset for success? It starts with one fundamental truth: your thoughts create your reality. Every single thought you have shapes your future. Every belief you hold is either pushing you forward or holding you back. You need to become hyper-aware of what's going on in your head. Ask yourself: What kind of thoughts are you feeding your mind? Are they rooted in abundance or scarcity, possibility or limitation? Are they thoughts of success or fear of failure?

Because here's the hard truth: if you keep telling yourself you can't do something, guess what? You're right. You can't. It's not because you're incapable—it's because you've already decided you're not. But if you flip the script—if you start telling yourself you can, if you start believing in your ability to figure things out, to overcome obstacles, to achieve the impossible—your entire world begins to shift.

When you adopt this mindset, you'll start seeing opportunities you never noticed before. Solutions to problems that once seemed insurmountable will suddenly reveal themselves. This is the power of a success mindset.

Some people might say, "But what about reality? What about the facts?" Here's something you need to understand about so-called facts: they're overrated. Facts change. The four-minute mile was once a fact—until Roger Bannister decided it wasn't. People couldn't fly—that was a fact—until the Wright brothers made their first flight in 1903. Your so-called "facts" are simply limitations you've accepted as truth. Even scientific facts change over time due to new insights and discoveries. One major evolving understanding is the concept of epigenetics, which explores how environmental factors can influence gene expression without altering the DNA sequence. Until about 20 years ago, it was assumed that everything was determined by genes.

However, scientists have now realized that epigenetic changes play a significant role in how our genes are expressed. This means that our lifestyle, diet, and even stress levels can influence how genes are "turned on or off." In other words, genes determine far less about who you, your behavior are and how your life unfolds than previously believed.

The most successful people don't accept the world as it is—they see the world as it could be and then they make it happen.

That's the mindset you need to cultivate. You need to believe, without a shadow of a doubt, that you can create a new reality. And you can, but it starts with acting like the person who already has.

This mindset shift won't happen overnight. It's like building a muscle—it takes consistent effort, repetition, and sometimes, discomfort. But that discomfort? That's where growth happens. Each time you challenge your beliefs, push past your comfort zone, and train your mind to focus on what's possible, you're taking one more step toward living your best life.

Start by auditing your thoughts. Pay attention to how you speak to yourself. When you catch yourself thinking negatively, stop and challenge that thought. Replace it with one that empowers you. Surround yourself with success—read books, listen to podcasts, and immerse yourself in an environment that fosters growth. But don't just consume—apply. Knowledge without action is useless. Taking action, even if it's just a small step each day, creates momentum. Momentum reshapes your beliefs about what's possible. And once you start to believe, you'll find there's nothing you can't achieve. The only thing stopping you from living your best life is you. Start acting as if you're already there, and soon enough, you will be.

What Do You Really Want?

That's about it for this part on mindset. I hope you've gained greater insight into your mindset, where your thoughts and beliefs originated, and how you can reprogram your conditioning. I've also explained the kinds of thoughts that get in the way of doing what you really want to do. But the big question still remains: What do you really want?

What would you like to sow and reap? What would you do if time and money were not an issue? What would your life look like if you could shape it differently today? What would you want to change? Or are things fine the way they are? I've asked thousands of people these questions and heard thousands of answers. We all have our own unique desires and dreams.

Perhaps you want to travel around the world and explore the beauty of our planet. Maybe you want to start your own business. It could be that things are going well for you and that you're looking to achieve financial independence. Or are you looking for purpose, satisfaction, or perhaps more peace of mind? If you're young and still have your whole life ahead of you, you may not yet know what you want. I hope this book will then give you direction. Perhaps you've reached a point where you really want to chart an entirely new course in life. It doesn't matter. The important thing is that you discover what you want, what makes you happy. If that's not sufficiently clear, you'll have to do some exploring.

Ask yourself questions that will give you direction, and keep going until you can write down in clear terms what you want. Make it so concrete that you can see the image of the outcome in front of you in your mind's eye. Or better yet, draw it or make a vision board, a collage of images that depicts your goal or dream. You could collect and paste photos. Or put together a collection of images on your computer screen. When you look at these every day and feel genuine emotion about them, the images are received by your subconscious.

It could also be that you have desires and dreams, but you have no idea where to start to make them come true. Or you've buried them because someone told you they were unrealistic and unattainable. Are you fearful of what others will think?

When I was convinced a job in radio was in the cards for me, almost everyone told me it would be impossible. When I announced I was starting an innovative media company, I was advised against it. People criticized my idea of taking an indefinite sabbatical because they thought I was much too young to stop working. When

I decided to write books, people made no secret of their doubts. And when I wanted to start speaking about the art of living and mindset, the leading speakers' agencies weren't exactly banging down my door.

Now, several years on, I have spoken in front of tens of thousands of people, and my books have sold almost a million copies and have been translated into several languages. Selling my companies gave me financial freedom, which made it possible to fulfill my dreams: to live on my yacht and enjoy the sea, sun, and peace. And a new dream: building a small "castle" on our wonderful estate.

None of this came automatically. Every reward was the result of hard work, a lot of sacrifices, perseverance, and unwavering self-confidence. And, of course, I had to take risks because every success comes with those. I had to endure humiliation, I was laughed at, and along the way, I lost. But I never gave up.

Know that the road to success is not a smoothly paved one, nor does it have a red carpet. In truth, it can be quite the opposite. It's a bumpy road with pitfalls, risks, and obstacles. You may even fall prey to your own hubris and foolhardiness. On the other hand, it's perhaps not surprising that almost everyone who has achieved really major successes has first had to overcome massive setbacks. When borne of necessity or unrestrained desire, certain forces emerge that can grow into invincibility.

The lesson is clear: if you really want something, don't let anything or anyone stand in your way. Don't let random, unsubstantiated opinions knock you off balance. If criticism of others easily sways you, you let them take control of your thoughts. It means you lack self-esteem and self-confidence. And as a result, your stance in life is wobbly, and you are easily thrown off kilter. So, work on your self-esteem, your self-confidence, get that energy level up, and live your life by your own personal rules. In other words, train your personal mastery.

Having said that, it is wise to take expert advice to heart and follow it. Do comprehensive research before you start. Find a good role model; prepare thoroughly. And regardless of what you want, make sure you start with the end in mind. The complete step-by-step plan can be found in Part IV of this book.

One last piece of advice on this topic. When you invest time, money, attention, and love but can't live with the possibility of loss, don't take action. Do this only when you're able to accept the possibility of loss; otherwise, feelings of fear will keep tripping you up or leading you astray.

What do you really want? Take plenty of time to think about that. It's an important question that will bring guidance to your daily life.

Let me give you this example to illustrate. Imagine you won the lottery. A silly game where you literally cast your fate to the wind. Yet millions of people participate in lotteries in the hopes of winning that one big cash prize. Maybe you, too, are hoping for a winning ticket so you can make all your dreams come true. Imagine winning that dream prize today: 365 days a year off and a disposable income of $100,000 a month. What would you do then? What would you do if virtually anything were possible?

It's my firm conviction that the reason we're here is to learn, grow, make a positive contribution to society, help others, love each other, and above all, enjoy. Enjoy the beauty of nature, the sun, and the wind; enjoy a glass of good wine, delicious food, and all the little things that make each day so precious. Be grateful for your health and for all the opportunities that come your way and enjoy all those moments you have the privilege of sharing with the people you love.

But to live such a beautiful life, it is still you who has to be the one to take action. And before you can do that, you need to think about that important question: How do you really want to make your life meaningful?

The Keys to Mastering Your Mindset

- **The power of thought:** What you focus on becomes your reality. Understanding and controlling your mindset is essential for personal mastery.

- **Personal operating system:** Like a computer, your mind has been programmed with various thought patterns, some of which are beneficial, while others may be flawed or limiting.

- **Conditioning and paradigms:** Your mindset is the result of years of conditioning and programming based on experiences, beliefs, and information. Changing that programming requires awareness and deliberate effort.

- **Rewrite your story:** To change your life, you need to change your mindset. This involves identifying limiting beliefs, breaking free from old thought patterns, and creating new, empowering ones.

- **Fear is just a thought:** Fear often holds you back, but it is a creation of your mind. By identifying your fears and understanding their roots, you can overcome them and move forward.

- **Breaking through limiting beliefs:** Limiting beliefs act as invisible barriers that prevent you from reaching your goals. Identifying and replacing them with positive, empowering beliefs is key to personal transformation.

- **Mindset and emotions:** Your emotions are directly influenced by your thoughts. Mastering your mindset allows you to manage your emotions, leading to a more balanced and fulfilled life.

- **Visualization and the law of attraction:** Visualizing your goals and aligning your thoughts with what you want to achieve attracts the right opportunities and outcomes into your life.

- **Focus on what you want:** Instead of dwelling on what you don't want, focus your attention on positive outcomes. Clear, specific goals and strong intentions drive success.
- **Take action:** The quality of your life is determined by the actions you take. Once you've reprogrammed your mindset, consistent, purposeful action is necessary to manifest your goals and dreams.

*"Success is no coincidence.
It is the result of your mindset
and following a focused strategy."*

PART

IV

The Strategy

The Roadmap to Success and Happiness

SUCCESS IS THE result of the way you think. Belief in yourself is your greatest power, and you have to be convinced that you can achieve whatever you want. That's one side of the equation. You've examined the philosophy of your mindset, your self-limiting thoughts, and how to reprogram them. The other side of the equation consists of being resourceful, good preparation, a lot of practice, hard work, and a little bit of luck. That's the formula for success in almost anything. So now it's time for action.

The next step on the path to your goal is to draw up a roadmap. What do you have to do, and what path do you have to take to reach your goal? Making your dream come true isn't about just thinking, it's about doing it. Doing is the key to success. No action, no results. I too often see dreams remaining pipe dreams because no action gets taken.

What you need is a manual, a step-by-step plan. The strategy I'm going to explain to you in this final section has been proven effective. But before you can get started on it, it's important to do a thorough self-knowledge check and to be aware of any of your pitfalls: the causes of failure.

Self-Knowledge Check: Get to Know Yourself Better

You're going to do a self-knowledge check by means of a series of questions and assignments. They are not easy, though immensely helpful to better understand yourself. Take time for them and give them all your attention.

The thought process and answers arising from the check will give you insights that will help you better understand who you are and where you are now. This analysis is crucial because you need this knowledge before you understand where you are, where you want to go, what you need to get there, and what's holding you back right now. You are always the starting point, and from there, you can take the first steps on your journey.

These Are the Three Essential Questions

1. Where do you want to go? (goal)
2. Where are you now? (starting point)
3. What's standing between you and your goal? In other words, what's holding you back, and what do you need to get to where you want to be? (obstacles)

I have a few assignments for you so you can answer these questions properly. These assignments are most effective when you write the answers down on paper. Just thinking about them isn't enough. I did that, too, the first few times I read *Think and Grow Rich*. But from the moment I started answering all the questions and assignments in the book by writing them down, my insights changed, and so did the results I got.

Reading is one thing. Studying it makes a massive difference. But doing it—that is, thinking about things attentively and then writing them down—can completely change the course of the rest of your life.

Take your time. Listen closely to the answer that comes to mind, and don't look for the answer using reason, but rather go within and feel it. Answer the questions honestly, based on your feelings, emotions, and thoughts over the past four weeks. Listen to what bubbles to the surface. It's not a test, but a self-knowledge check meant to generate insights. It's about you, both privately and professionally, and everything you do and experience on a daily basis. Answer the questions as specifically as possible, and write your answers down.

Assignment 1

1. What thoughts have been keeping you preoccupied lately?
2. What questions keep you up at night?
3. What emotions do you experience most frequently?
4. What do you believe triggers these questions, thoughts, and emotions?
5. On a scale of 1–10, what is your personal happiness score?
6. On a scale of 1–10, what is your personal success score?
7. Why do you do what you do, both privately and at work?
8. What do you really want (personally, physically, professionally, financially, and health-wise)?
9. What is preventing you from doing what you really want to do?

Assignment 2

These nine questions can help you on your way to figuring out what you like and what suits you.

1. What makes you happy?
2. What do you love doing so much that you never want to stop doing it?
3. What are you good at?
4. What have been your happiest moments?
5. How do you want other people to see you?
6. What do you take pleasure in?
7. What do you find important in life?
8. What are you grateful for?
9. Who are you? Describe your personality and your behavior, including your good and bad traits.

Assignment 3

Ask three people who know you well to describe in writing how they see you. Ask them to talk about your qualities. What are you good and less good at? Have them describe your behavior. Ask for honest answers. It shouldn't all be praise; they should also note the less-positive things. In fact, you can use those insights to help you improve yourself.

Assignment 4

This is a good exercise to gain more insight into what you like and what direction to start looking at when it comes to work, relationships, where you live, and ultimately, your best life.

Take two sheets of paper. Write the word "positive (+)" at the top of one sheet and "negative (−)" at the top of the other. Describe everything that makes you happy and what you enjoy on the "positive" sheet. And on the "negative" sheet, write down everything you don't like, all that doesn't make you happy. Don't limit it to professional things. You might notice that there is a relation with your personal values on the positive sheet and little connection on the negative sheet.

Some examples: Do you like living in sunny, warm areas, or do you prefer to live where it's cold? Do you like working with people, or not? Does working with animals make you feel good? Do you like social life much, or not? Do you like wasting time chit-chatting, or do you prefer to read or learn something? Do you like working 9-to-5, or do you prefer the freedom of a flexible schedule? Do you like complex people, or do you prefer to stay away from them? Would you like to work inside or outside? In a team, or by yourself? Also write down what has your interest and what does not; what do you hate and what do you love? Writing it all down will bring you clarity and it shows you a direction where you will find meaning and purpose.

> *"People who are almost always successful*
> *and people who regularly fail*
> *generally do the exact opposite things."*

The Law of Inverse Proportionality

Success and failure may be opposites, but I've discovered that in terms of patterns, they're nearly the same. People who are successful and people who regularly fail generally do the exact opposite things. I call this the law of inverse proportionality, or opposites. There's a really clear pattern here.

Where the growth-oriented mindset plays to win, the static thinker plays not to lose. One thinks big, the other thinks big problems. And while one sees problems in everything, the other knows how to come up with solutions for everything. People who have a positive mental attitude often see opportunities instead of problems. People with receptive and positive mindsets admire successful people and wonder what they can learn from them; people with static mindsets have all kinds of judgments about others before they've ever even met them.

There are also major differences in communication skills. People who navigate through life successfully are predominantly positive-minded, are open to other ways of thinking, are fascinating to listen to, are interested, and are less likely to speak negatively of others. People with more static mindsets are more likely to experience problems, are more likely to see the world from a negative perspective, can't always express themselves well, are more likely to have conflicts with others, are less likely to be open to learning new things, and tend to speak negatively of others.

One saves or invests, and the other easily spends too much money on consumer goods. Successful people have self-discipline. Those who cannot keep agreements with themselves will never achieve success. People who achieve structural success are willing to work hard and persevere, while others "would like that too" but don't generally take action or give up too quickly. Finally, the growth-oriented mind allows itself to be rewarded for results, while the static mindset is mainly paid for time.

Do you see the pattern? A given action, a given mindset, your way of thinking and doing, leads to a given outcome. That outcome is rarely a surprise; it's a simple formula. When you do the opposite of what you want, you can almost always expect the opposite result.

When we look at major sports heroes, we see that mentality is often the decisive factor in their long-lasting success. Michael Jordan is one of the best basketball players of all time. He wasn't a natural talent, but he was probably one of the hardest-working athletes ever. He was kicked off the college team and rejected by the first two NBA teams who could've picked him, but he didn't let that discourage him. He continuously worked to improve his talent. "I've missed more than nine thousand shots in my career. I've lost almost three hundred games. Twenty-six times, I've been trusted to take the game-winning shot and missed. I've failed over and over again. And that is why I succeed," was Michael Jordan's conclusion. Like every top athlete, he trained extremely hard, but he always learned from his mistakes and kept working at things. According to Jordan, success originates in the mind. Mental toughness and mental resilience count for more than just talent and physical prowess.

The legendary Muhammad Ali didn't fit the image of the perfect boxer. According to experts, he wasn't a natural talent either. He was fast, but he didn't have the body of a great champion. What he did have was a brilliant attitude. His invincible spirit was his superpower.

In her TED talk, Professor Carol Dweck explains that the belief that one can improve serves as a wellspring of personal strength. In her 30 years of research, she has been able to demonstrate that the view you choose to have of yourself strongly influences the way you lead your life. This mindset can determine whether you become the person you want to be. The growth-oriented mindset has its origins in the belief that one can work on oneself by making an effort. According to Napoleon Hill in *Think and Grow Rich*, faith is the most important alchemist of the mind. Your way of thinking determines who you are and what you do.

Many people who do what they really enjoy have a growth-oriented mindset. People who follow their desire live from a place of passion. Perhaps they don't even initially set out to reach the top. But because of their drive, passion, and perseverance, this is often a side effect of their efforts. What's worth noting is that it's often the people with a static mindset who strive more for respect and appreciation, yet it's precisely that attitude that stands in the way of progress and change.

Only lasting development and growth lead to success and happiness. You grow by stretching beyond your comfort zone time and again. You have to push your own boundaries. That means you have to do things that make you feel uncomfortable. Some things can feel uncomfortable when you first do them, or you might feel insecure about them beforehand. In hindsight, it's usually not as tough as you thought it would be, and the more often you do it, the easier it gets.

For a period in my life, I was lazy and dumb. Then one day I had enough of the spare tire around my waist. I wanted an attractive and healthy body again. Not only to look good, but as I got older, I've noticed that a strong and vital body is a must to live healthy and happy until the end.

So, on the advice of the chiropractor, my then-girlfriend Cindy, and the mirror, I found myself in a gym for the first time in 25 years. I needed professional help and made an appointment with a personal trainer. There I was, not entirely at ease, in a trendy gym where well-known TV personalities and professional sports heroes were seriously training and body shaping.

In the first few weeks, sticking to the intensive workout schedule was nothing but suffering, pain, and exhaustion. A couple of weeks later, I started enjoying the workouts more and got a bit of support from the mirror, which was reflecting the results of the workouts. My body was getting noticeably stronger, and the more I worked out, the less back pain and other little physical ailments I had. Another bonus was that I started feeling more energetic and alive, and automatically started drinking less alcohol and eating healthier. It may sound logical and obvious, yet we don't always do what we know is good for us.

If we look at the results of the tens of thousands of participants in my programs, it's quite evident that most of them start maintaining a much healthier lifestyle. We regularly receive messages from people who've lost serious weight within a few months and then keep that weight off. I myself lost 45 pounds of

> *"Success is nothing more than a few simple disciplines, practiced every day. While failure is simply a few errors in judgment, repeated every day.*
> *It is the cumulative weight of our disciplines and our judgments that leads us to either fortune or failure."*
> — **Jim Rohn**

ballast, and since then, I've kept my weight at around 184 pounds. The latter—long-term success—is especially important, or in this case, a balanced, healthy lifestyle. This also goes for participants who've abruptly stopped using drugs, drinking, smoking, and other unhealthy habits, including negative thinking.

Anyone can stop temporarily. Rigorously changing your lifestyle, however, requires awareness, discipline, desire and/or necessity, perseverance, and a clear mind—in other words, a positive mental attitude. That's vastly different than positive thinking, hoping, and wishing.

Most new activities and behavior patterns initially feel uncomfortable or even generate resistance. But if you continue to hang in there and train yourself in being disciplined, you'll stretch beyond your comfort zone and step up your perseverance. You'll get satisfaction from your new mindset and behavior. And satisfaction is a fertile breeding ground for success and happiness.

Twelve Causes of Failure

To explain the law of reverse proportionality a bit further, I've written down 12 common causes of failure for you. By knowing what not to do, you'll increase your chance of success by definition. Success and failure are both the result of a particular way of thinking and subsequent actions—or the absence thereof.

When you consistently do the opposite of what leads to success, you will naturally encounter failure. This means that failure is rarely the result of bad luck; it usually comes down to using the wrong "strategy." In both cases, patterns of thought and action can be identified. Success is often the result of the daily application of simple, effective disciplines. Similarly, failure is the result of repeated mistakes, rooted in faulty assumptions and judgments. The repetition of poor habits brings failure just as surely as the repetition of good habits brings success. Following are the 12 most common causes of failure:

1. **Lack of a concrete goal**
   When you don't have a clear goal, you wander aimlessly through life. You don't just have one goal in life—you have short- and long-term goals. Many people, however, don't engage in setting and achieving concrete goals. Whether the goals are big or small, if you don't know exactly where you're going or what you want to achieve, you won't be motivated to use your time and energy wisely. And without direction, you risk ending up somewhere you don't want to be.

2. **Lack of targeted attention (focus)**
   Concentrate on what you really want. Focus on the few, not the many. It's impossible to stay focused on lots of different things. People with a thousand ideas rarely put even one into practice. Fragmented attention leads to reduced capacity, confusion, and loss of energy. Success means setting priorities. Determine what you think is important, and spend all your time on it. It's about focused attention. Do one thing really well—not all kinds of things halfway or not at all. You can't specialize in everything. Make informed choices. Determine what you want very clearly. Waste as little time as possible, and don't allow yourself to be distracted by anything and everything. Aim straight for your goal.

3. **Fear**
   Fear is a deceptive enemy that strikes when you're mentally weak. In the section titled "Fear is just a thought,"

I mentioned the basic fears that prevent you from doing what you really want to do. What are you really afraid of? Know that fear especially arises when you don't know what you want and don't have a clear goal. If you notice that fear is holding you back, ask yourself this question: What's the worst thing that can happen? Don't make it worse in your head than it is. See things as they really are; stick to the facts.

4. **Indecisiveness**
    Indecisiveness is a common cause of failure. It often leads to doubt, and doubt fosters anxiety. People who hesitate often feel unlucky, but in reality, their indecision causes missed opportunities. The more choices you have, the harder it is to decide. Indecision paralyzes you, and over time, it creates a life of missed opportunities.

    "I may be wrong, but I'm never in doubt" is what my mentor Dan Peña always says. Successful people seldom to never have doubts. They make quick, well-considered decisions and don't easily change their minds.

    Taking control of your life requires making decisions— and owning the consequences. If you don't choose, someone else or time will choose for you. Are you afraid of making the wrong decision? Asking good questions will help clarify things. Don't overcomplicate matters, and trust your intuition. Remember, "One day" leads to a town called nowhere. Waiting for the "right moment" is like waiting for a bus that never comes. Now is always the right time.

5. **Lack of self-discipline**
    Many people are naturally lazy and prefer to take the easy road. We'd rather look good, have a great partner, and earn a lot, but not do too much for it. That's not how things work. Discipline and perseverance are the foundation of every success. If you give up before you reach your goal,

you'll never succeed. Even though this sounds fairly obvious, I see time and again that a lot of people bail out prematurely. If you want to win, you'll have to train intensively and for a long time. Many people give up halfway, and only a few are driven enough to reach the finish line. No complaining, no bellyaching. It's a matter of taking action. Discipline is self-control. That means you make agreements with yourself and stick to them.

6. Lack of passion

Passion is the fuel of the imagination, the driving force you need to make your dreams come true. Passion originates deep within you. It is boundless enthusiasm. It is an infectious energy that radiates outwards onto the people around you. What you do doesn't matter but do it with passion and attention.

Cindy and I were at a restaurant a few years back where a young lady waiting tables was walking around with a disinterested air the whole evening. Even though there weren't so many guests, it took forever for us to get served. She was more interested in her phone than the guests. And then she showed up with the wrong dishes. When it came time to pay, she was really indignant because I didn't give her a tip. She started telling me that she was poorly paid and that her income was largely dependent on tips. I gave her the following advice: "You could earn loads of extra money if you smiled a bit more and were friendly. Look at guests when you communicate with them, listen to them, pay attention to them, be sincere, and at least serve them what they've ordered. If you had done that, I would have rewarded you with a good tip." That genuine attention has to come from within you and flow from your passion. If the service industry isn't for you, then find a job you can put your heart and soul into. If you aren't driven by a burning desire, you can't rise above yourself and achieve great things.

7. **Lack of perseverance**

   A lot of people get off to an enthusiastic start but don't finish anything. They tend to give up at the first sign of failure. But if you keep going until something succeeds, you almost can't fail. Winners never quit, and quitters never win. The basis of perseverance is willpower, an essential factor in transforming desires into desired outcomes. Combining your intense desire with perseverance creates a virtually invincible source of strength.

8. **Negative behavior**

   People with a negative attitude also project a negative vibe. That's why they don't get far with others; others take notice. And in order to achieve success, you have to work with others. No one ever becomes successful all on their own. Maintain a positive mental attitude. That's much more than just positive thinking. You have to be positive, think positive, and act positive. If you're genuinely positive in life, you'll notice that your energy, the vibration you put out there, your spark, will automatically jump over to others. A powerful, positive vibe will attract people and situations that can help you on your path.

9. **Limiting beliefs**

   You can never be bigger than your own thoughts. Your thoughts are your greatest limitation. Self-limiting thoughts put us behind imaginary bars. Many people are stuck in these invisible prisons that they themselves have created with their emotional blockades and limiting thoughts. Magic can be found outside your comfort zone, but as long as you don't dare to cross the threshold of your front door, you'll never enjoy the wondrous outside world. Unfortunately, most people have been programmed with self-limiting beliefs from an early age. We've been told what is and isn't possible. If you think something isn't possible, then it won't be. If you think it is, then that will be the case. But that must be an absolute conviction. If you fool yourself by pretending to believe in something that you're not really convinced of deep inside, then it will not work.

10. **Lack of ambition**

Our school systems and society are geared toward mediocrity. Many people are afraid of being "better" than others, afraid of criticism, and deep inside, also afraid of success. Which is logical since no one prepares us for success. On the contrary, putting your head above the parapet isn't always appreciated. Those around you would then rather pull you back down to the safety of mediocrity.

If you don't want to take a step forward in your life, you'll stay where you are forever. That's great, as long as you're satisfied with that. If you want more, you'll have to make decisions that lift you above the mundane.

That lack of ambition that a lot of people have is actually quite unnatural. It's not that you always have to be the best or the most successful, but our lives are part of nature, and nature is always in motion. Nature always makes use of potential. The trees don't stop growing halfway because that's good enough. Caterpillars don't think "Make all that effort to become a butterfly? I can't do it anyway. Nah, I'll just keep on crawling." And yet this is what many people unfortunately do; they crawl through life while they could become butterflies. While they could be showing their beauty to the world. While they could be spreading their wings to fly.

11. **Lack of self-esteem**

Lack of self-esteem is one of the most common barriers. People with a lack of self-esteem or self-respect usually suffer from multiple causes of failure: too little or no self-confidence; no self-discipline; indecisiveness; and thinking in limitations, but also anxiousness, uncertainty and negative behavior. They continually underestimate themselves. They're afraid to be seen. They have a low energy level, and this creates negative and unbalanced emotions. They hold themselves in low esteem, so they ask for little and are frequently underpaid, often leading them to feel wronged as a result.

The biggest cause of lack of self-esteem is not believing in yourself. Believing in yourself is your greatest strength, and not believing in yourself is your greatest weakness. When you don't believe in yourself, you surrender your power to others, to their expectations and to "what others think." Such a fragile and weak self-image is the result of years of negative conditioning.

If you lack self-esteem, then you also have little self-confidence. And that means you hesitate easily and don't dare to make choices. And it is choices that determine the direction of your life. It works the other way around too. If you don't know exactly what you want to do, you can't determine how to do it, and uncertainty will strike. To get more clarity, you first have to ask good questions. That brings insight and gives you more self-confidence. And from that self-confidence, your self-esteem will grow.

Finally, one more thing I'd like to mention. Often, when someone considers themselves a perfectionist, it is insecurity in disguise, a lack of self-esteem. Perfection is an illusion. If you're not able to judge when something is good enough, you fall into the trap of perfectionism. To overcome being a perfectionist, improve your self-confidence and self-esteem.

12. Excuses

If your excuses are always bigger than your goals and dreams, you'll never be able to make your dreams a reality.

People who are not as successful as they would like to be or who feel like they're the victims of everything often share a common characteristic: they always have an excuse on hand to justify their failures. They make quick use of the word "if." "If I had more money …" "If I'd had the same opportunities …" "If I were lucky for once …" "If I had more time …" "If the circumstances were better …" If, if, if.

If you have the courage to face the truth and be honest with yourself, you'll throw all your excuses overboard and take responsibility for your own life and actions. The magic word is "do." In the *Tao Te Ching*, Lao Tzu uses the legendary words: "A journey of a thousand miles begins with a single step."

When should you take that first step? The time is now. The 12 causes summarized here are finely interwoven and lead toward failure. But they also have positive counterparts that form the recipe for success. If it's success that you're after, then you have to follow the path, or strategy, that leads toward it.

> "Every time you climb a mountain,
> you have to start at the bottom.
> How good you are and how high
> the mountain is, doesn't matter.
> You have to start at the bottom."

My Way of Thinking and Acting

The recipe for a happy and successful life is simple, but such a life doesn't just magically happen. It requires consistent, focused effort. Through the power of repetition, your subconscious mind will gradually embed these principles into your internal operating system. Reading and studying alone aren't enough. To truly benefit from the philosophy and strategy outlined in this book, you must turn those words into purposeful, targeted action. That's why I want to emphasize the significant value of engaging with my teaching programs, as they provide the practical tools and guidance needed to fully implement these strategies in your life.

The strategy I've discovered over the years is highly effective. It's a way of thinking and acting that I started applying unconsciously over 35 years ago. I began to notice that success followed a discernible pattern. At first, it was just with myself, but as I studied other successful people, I saw the same patterns emerging. Success, I realized, isn't random. That's why you'll often hear me say that success is not a coincidence; it's a science. After countless moments of trial and error, picking myself up after failures, celebrating successes, and learning from my teachers, I distilled my experiences into a 12-step strategy.

This strategy helped me, often unconsciously, to become a renowned DJ, and consciously when I built my media company. I applied it to my sailing trips, writing my books, and setting up our publishing company, which has now sold over a million books. The same method guided the creation of the Meditation Moments app, our Mastermind Academy, and everything I do as a writer, speaker, and teacher. For Cindy and me, this approach has become second nature, our way of life.

It isn't rocket science, but you must fully understand it to make it work for you. I like to compare it to building a house. First, you envision what kind of house you want. You might browse online for inspiration, create a mood board, and shape your vision of the perfect home. Next, you hire an architect to bring your ideas to life with a detailed plan. You'll also need a contractor, skilled laborers, permits, materials, and the right tools. Of course, you'll need land—where will you build? What kind of environment do you want, and what view will you enjoy? Throughout this process, you must calculate costs and consider financing. Once all these elements are aligned, you're ready to formalize the plan.

With a clear plan, you move to execution. You start with the foundation, pour the concrete base, build sturdy walls, and create stability before adding floors and the roof. Plumbing, wiring, and finishing touches come afterward. The process requires focus and foresight—visualizing the finished product while concentrating on the specific steps needed at each moment. Step by step, brick by brick, you build toward the final result.

Writing a book offers another perfect example. When I decided to write my first novel, my goal was clear: to have a hundred thousand readers and land a top-10 spot on the bestseller list. I began with the end goal in mind, but my writing teacher, Mr. B., reminded me to focus on the basics first— writing a great story. He was right. It wasn't the time to worry about selling the book. He knew that many stories never make it beyond a computer screen or, at best, become mediocre manuscripts.

I took his advice and dedicated myself to improving my craft, but I also kept my strategy in mind. While focusing on the quality of the writing, I simultaneously applied my 12-step strategy to guide me toward my ultimate goal. I'll share the details of how I did that later.

Is the 12-step strategy the only way to succeed? Certainly not. There are many paths to success, but this approach to thinking and doing has been around for ages. Great leaders, visionaries, and countless successful individuals have used similar methods to achieve their goals. I'm sharing this knowledge with you, enhanced by my personal experiences, so that you too can apply it to your journey.

The 12-Step Strategy

Step 1: Master your mindset

Step 2: Personal mastery

Step 3: Set clear and concrete goals

Step 4: Visualize the end result

Step 5: Write down your affirmations

Step 6: Have role models

Step 7: Research before you begin

Step 8: Create a strategic plan

Step 9: Create your dream team

Step 10: Move before you're ready

Step 11: Do whatever it takes

Step 12: Focus on your goals

The 12-step strategy I'm going to explain to you is a method that I developed based on different elements. The fundamentals are based on what I've learned from my business mentor Dan Peña. These I've combined with the principles from *Think and Grow Rich* and the many lessons I learned from my other teachers and my own experiences. You can apply the strategy to many realms. It is important to take the steps on your own, so that they become your guiding principles, your way of life.

When I began explaining this strategy years ago, it consisted of 10 steps. The first step was to set a concrete and clear goal. Yet over time, I discovered that some people were getting stuck and not achieving their goals. When I examined the causes of that, I found that it almost always had to do with not having the right mindset. Something about their way of thinking was faulty. Or something was wrong with their personal mastery. From then on, I started paying greater attention to personal mastery and to mindset, which is why I added those first two steps. Step 1 and

Step 2 establish the necessary foundation. After that, it's about following and implementing the rest of the strategy. That makes it absolutely possible to turn your dreams and desires into reality.

Step 1: Master Your Mindset

Before you can successfully implement the 12 steps, your first priority is to master your mindset. As I explained in Part III, reprogramming your thoughts is essential to break free from fear and uncertainty.

In short, who you are and what you do are direct outcomes of your thoughts. Your conditioning—your internal operating system—shapes your behavior. It's crucial to recognize your beliefs and understand where they come from. By examining the thought patterns that have guided your life, you gain insight into how they influence your present reality.

If things in your life aren't going the way you want, it's time to shift your mindset. Change your thoughts and beliefs, and your life will follow.

Mastering your mindset is not a one-time effort—it's an ongoing practice. It requires developing awareness of your thought patterns and consciously choosing to cultivate positive, productive beliefs that support the life you want to create. As you strengthen this practice, your mindset becomes your greatest tool for navigating challenges and achieving success.

Remember, everything starts in your mind. Shift your mindset, and you'll shift your life.

> *"You become great by growing, learning,*
> *and improving yourself a little bit every day."*

Step 2: Personal Mastery

Personal mastery is the key to unlocking your full potential, forming the foundation for every other step in this 12-step strategy. Without mastering your mindset, managing your energy, refining your communication skills, building your self-esteem, and developing self-discipline, any other progress will be limited.

Personal mastery isn't a skill you grasp overnight. It's a process—a lifelong journey of self-awareness, growth, and refinement. It's about living consciously and consistently striving to improve yourself, one small step at a time.

At its core, personal mastery begins with your mindset (Step 1). From there, it expands into other crucial areas like your energy levels, emotional intelligence, self-discipline, and how you communicate with the world around you. It's about learning how to harness your inner power to reach new heights.

What Is Personal Mastery?

To achieve personal mastery is to reach a level of self-awareness, self-control, and purpose-driven action that allows you to maximize your potential. The most successful people I've encountered share certain traits. They have an undeniable clarity about what they want, unwavering discipline to pursue it, and a mindset that stays resilient even in the face of challenges.

They follow a path driven by passion, which gives them energy and satisfaction. Their sense of purpose allows them to rise above distractions and obstacles. They possess self-confidence, self-esteem, discipline, resilience, and an extraordinary ability to focus. What also strikes me is the simplicity of how they think and act, as does their resourcefulness. They don't get hung up on problems but are instead almost always able to come up with creative solutions. They rarely hesitate, make quick choices, and are resolute. In general, they're full of energy and keep going when others give up. They're usually positive people with above-average communication skills. They trust their intuition, they dare to take risks, and they work hard—sometimes extremely hard—but they love what they do.

The Path of Constant Improvement

Most successful people invest heavily in their personal development. They don't stop learning—they learn from everything: books, experiences, setbacks, and the people they meet. Personal mastery is not a destination, but a journey of constant refinement. If you do the same, you'll be able to get the most out of yourself without exhausting yourself. And you'll be positioned to live your best life. Whatever goal you set for yourself and no matter how brilliant your plans are, you'll never achieve anything if you don't work on yourself.

Satisfaction, success, and happiness are the result of growth. To become the best version of yourself, you first need to know where you're at now. To be aware of that, you need to live consciously. From there, you can work on yourself. Personal mastery is about making sure you are always growing. It's about reaching new levels of awareness and performance in every aspect of life: physically, mentally, emotionally, and spiritually.

The Eight Pillars of Personal Mastery

To achieve personal mastery, you need to develop in all key areas of your life. To achieve success, you must work on yourself—constantly. Satisfaction, happiness, and success are direct results of your growth. But to grow, you need to understand where you are now. You must assess yourself honestly. This is what living consciously means. You can only make progress if you are aware of your current physical, mental, emotional, and spiritual state.

I've identified eight key elements that make up what I call the *Art of Living Pyramid*, which is rooted in Maslow's hierarchy of needs. Each of these elements is critical to living a balanced, fulfilled life. These elements are:

1. **Health and vitality** – Your physical well-being and energy level form the foundation.

2. **Emotions** – Mastering your emotional state, managing stress, and nurturing positivity.
3. **Time Management** – Time management is crucial; learning to use time effectively ensures progress.
4. **Relationships** – Strong personal connections enrich your life and keep you grounded.
5. **Financial security** – Financial health reduces stress and provides freedom.
6. **Career** – Finding purpose and passion in your work leads to fulfillment.
7. **Relaxation** – Recharging your mind and body ensures longevity and resilience.
8. **Personal development** – Continuous learning and growth expand your mind and your potential.

All eight elements are important, but they are hierarchical and in a natural order. For example, vitality forms the base of the pyramid because without physical health and energy, it's impossible to sustain progress in other areas. To achieve a balanced life, you need to develop yourself in each area.

Let's break down each of these elements and why they matter.

Health and Vitality

Health and vitality are the foundation of everything else. If you are healthy in both mind and body, you won't be limited by physical restrictions, and you'll have the energy needed to pursue your goals. However, if you're constantly battling fatigue, illness, or mental burnout, it's much harder to make meaningful progress.

I've seen this firsthand in both my life and the lives of others. One of my closest friends has been living with a chronic illness for years. Despite her physical limitations, her mental strength and willpower are extraordinary. Instead of focusing on her limitations, she dedicates her energy to what she *can* do. This shift in focus has allowed her to live a fuller, more vibrant life than many people who are physically healthy but mentally restricted by negative thoughts.

Maintaining vitality is about more than just physical health. It's also about mental and emotional well-being. Jim Rohn once said, *"Take care of your body. It's the only place you have to live."* When you're full of energy, your thoughts are clearer, your emotions are more balanced, and you're more resilient when facing challenges.

Emotions

Once you've built a foundation of health, the next layer involves managing your emotions and time. Emotions are powerful—they can drive us to achieve great things, or they can derail us if left unchecked. Emotional intelligence is about recognizing and understanding your feelings and then using that awareness to guide your actions in a positive direction. When you manage your emotions effectively, you can turn them into a source of strength that pushes you forward, helping you stay focused and resilient even in challenging situations.

Time Management

Time management is also essential. We all have 24 hours in a day, but how we use those hours determines our success. If you don't manage your time well, you'll find yourself constantly overwhelmed and feeling like you're not making progress. This is why time management is one of the core skills in personal mastery.

Jim Rohn used to say, "Either you run the day, or the day runs you." Time is the one resource you can never get back, so it's crucial to use it wisely. By mastering time management, you take control of your life, reduce stress, and create space for important things. Successful people prioritize their time and focus on what matters most.

Relationships

Healthy relationships are crucial for happiness and support, but they take work. It's important to surround yourself with people who inspire you, who push you to be better, and who support your growth. Toxic relationships, on the other hand, can drain your energy and derail your progress. It's important to be intentional about the people you allow into your life. You are the average of the people you spend the most time with. Choose wisely, and make sure those around you lift you up rather than pull you down.

Financial Security

Financial security gives you the freedom to pursue your goals without the constant stress of worrying about money. But achieving financial security takes discipline. You must learn how to manage your resources wisely, save for the future, and invest in opportunities that align with your long-term vision.

Career

Success in your career doesn't happen overnight. It's often the result of hard work, passion, and persistence, built over time through countless hours of dedication. It's a gradual process that requires not only discipline but also a deep commitment to continuous learning and personal growth. You must be willing to put in the effort, even when things get tough, and stay committed to your path. True success also demands resilience—the ability to push forward through setbacks and challenges, all while maintaining a clear vision of your goals. Each step, no matter how small, brings you closer to the success you seek. Ultimately, it's your ability to remain focused and consistent that separates those who dream from those who achieve.

Relaxation

The final two elements—relaxation and personal development—are often overlooked but are critical for long-term success. Relaxation is necessary for recovery and rejuvenation. If you don't take time to rest, both physically and mentally, you'll burn out. This is why relaxation and stress management techniques like meditation, yoga, and mindful breathing are so important. These practices help clear your mind, improve focus, and increase your overall well-being.

Personal Development

Personal development is about continuously learning and growing. It's about pushing yourself beyond your comfort zone and expanding your skills and knowledge. Jim Rohn emphasized this, saying, *"Work harder on yourself than you do on your job."* The more you invest in yourself, the more capable you become of achieving your goals.

Assignment

Where are you now? Reviewing your current status. Consider each of these areas in your life. Rate yourself in each element from 0 to 10. This self-assessment will give you a clear understanding of where you're thriving and where there's room for improvement.

Ask yourself questions like:

- How healthy and vital do I feel?
- Do I manage my emotions, or do they manage me?

- Am I using my time wisely and effectively?
- Are my relationships fulfilling and meaningful?
- Am I financially secure, or is money a source of stress?
- Am I satisfied with my work or career?
- Do I take enough time to relax and recharge?
- Am I investing in my personal growth?

The areas where you score lower are the ones to focus on improving. Remember, personal mastery is about balanced growth—strengthening all areas of your life.

Master Your Communication

There are several more important skills that are very important in personal mastery. Some people have more natural aptitude for them than others, but all of these skills can be learned and developed. Let's start with communication skills.

Personal mastery is all about communication. It's how we connect with others, how we influence, how we build relationships, and how we lead. Yet communication is not only about speaking—it's equally about listening, understanding, and perceiving the world around you. To improve your communication skills, start by being mindful of how you speak and listen. Clear, direct communication helps avoid misunderstandings. Listening deeply to others—not just hearing the words but feeling the meaning behind them—can transform your relationships.

The quality of your communication may well be the most important skill that determines the course of your life. Dan Peña pointed this out to me years ago: how you come across to others and how you deal with them is of fundamental importance. All the successful people I know are masters in communication, each in their own way. They always have an interesting story, can captivate you for hours, and speak energetically and enthusiastically. They don't whine, aren't inconsistent, and don't exhaust you with verbal diarrhea.

Your whole life revolves around communication: how you say things, the way you look at them, how you respond, what you hear, what you see, and what you understand. That's why it's very important to always be crystal clear and straightforward in what you mean, what you say, and what you think. Are you a master in communication, or do you sometimes stumble and falter and often feel misunderstood? Have you ever wondered about that? Miscommunication and ambiguity are a source of disagreement, quarrels, and relationship problems.

Can you make what you want clear, and do you always achieve it, or are you continually at loggerheads with yourself? Connect with others if you want to bring a message across. When you talk with people, look them in the eye. Communication is about connection. I recently had a conversation with a student about a presentation. His teacher had some advice for students who found it scary to stand up and speak in front of the class. He said it was better to look out across the audience. I suddenly remembered I'd also been taught the same thing in school. Isn't that a strange way of teaching? The student had a problem, and instead of learning how to solve it, he was taught to avoid it.

If you don't dare look others in the eye, you lose contact and lack connection. That won't make you more confident as a student. It's a missed opportunity because it's precisely in school that students should learn about healthy communication. This skill is crucial—not only for your own life, but also for society as a whole. Communication is essential for our social lives, for tolerance, and for mutual respect.

There are two forms of communication: with others and with yourself. Most of the time, you carry out endless conversations with yourself inside your head. Negative self-talk can sabotage your efforts, while positive, constructive inner dialogue can propel you toward your goals. Dale Carnegie emphasized the importance of controlling your thoughts, reminding us that *"Our thoughts make us what we are."* Learning to master your internal communication is just as important as mastering your external communication.

Are you in charge of your thoughts and emotions, or do you allow yourself to be (mis)guided by your thoughts? For some people, this leads to an internal civil war. It's a battlefield with only one victim: you. If communication with yourself and others regularly leads to conflicts, ask yourself the following question: "How does that come about, and what can I do to improve my communication?" Could it have to do with how you see things, with the meaning you assign to them? We often form opinions too quickly on the basis of unreliable information or vague assumptions. Judgments and convictions fall under the umbrella of misleading communication. Don't think for others, don't judge too quickly, and don't talk about things if you haven't got all the facts.

Communication isn't only about broadcasting messages— talking, emailing, apping, gesturing. Listening is of even greater importance. Listening is a good example of focused attention. Listening is about perception and understanding. And to do that, you have to be in the now, fully present in the conversation.

"Have you ever thought about why you listen to someone else?" asked Indian spiritual teacher Krishnamurti at the beginning of a reading. What does that mean, listening to someone? Do you listen to get your own convictions confirmed, or do you want to learn something? Are you receptive, or just looking for arguments to support your own opinions? Listening is a life skill.

Communication seems natural and easy, but in practice, I regularly notice that many people struggle with it, often without realizing it themselves. We're taught how to talk and write. But communicating is something you have to learn.

My teacher taught me that a good interview or conversation doesn't need more than one very good question. The answer will automatically lead to follow-up questions. And then an interesting conversation ensues.

You have to determine beforehand what you want to know about the person you're talking to, and most of all, you have to listen attentively. Listen to what the other person really means, discover the information behind the spoken words. Listen not only with your ears, but with your whole body, and feel the other person's energy.

The tricky thing about listening attentively is that our mind starts to interfere. We start interpreting words and connecting them with associations from our own personal database. That's why many people can't listen properly. Their brains start processing other information and coloring things based on what they think they hear. If you are conversing with yourself in your thoughts, you can't listen to someone else properly. Intellect and emotion suppress feeling. As a result, the connection gets broken and unadulterated communication is lost. A lot of conflicts flow from this. You see it a lot in relationships. When you communicate only from a place of reason, without empathically listening, misunderstandings and problems are inevitable. And when emotions gain the upper hand, you completely lose the ability to perceive purely. Every word is then colored by your dominant emotion at that moment. By opening up and listening receptively from a loving state of being, you can make genuine contact with someone.

What can you do to improve your communication skills? First, consider what you want to say. What's your message? Stick to the essence, avoid unnecessary words and meaningless fluff, speak briefly and succinctly. Use your phone to record yourself. Listen back to hear how you speak, the words you use, whether you're credible and persuasive, or perhaps tedious and boring.

Listen carefully to the way you speak to see whether it's lively or monotonous. Read text messages and emails before you send them, and ask yourself whether your message is clear. We live in fast times and pay little attention to long, rambling messages. Your message should be to the point and come across well. Be clear in your communication, even when you're talking to yourself in your thoughts.

Find role models, people you admire for their communication skills. Observe and research what makes those people so good. How do they speak? How do they come across? Take note of their body language. Learn from it. And practice—a lot and often. Record videos of yourself, watch them, and correct yourself. Practice makes perfect.

Effective communication is essential for success. Whether in business, personal relationships, or leadership, mastering the art of communication is a powerful tool for success.

Developing Self-Esteem and Confidence

When you start mastering your mindset, boosting your energy levels, improving communication, and managing your time effectively, something powerful happens: your self-esteem grows. High self-esteem isn't about arrogance or overconfidence—it's about knowing your value and acting accordingly.

People with high self-esteem don't seek validation from others. They trust in their abilities and aren't afraid to make tough decisions or take risks. They are comfortable in their own skin and don't feel the need to put others down to elevate themselves.

Low self-esteem, on the other hand, can cripple your potential. It shows up as fear, procrastination, and an inability to assert yourself. If you constantly doubt your worth, you'll find it hard to make progress. To overcome low self-esteem, you need to consciously work on building your confidence and recognizing your strengths.

The word "self-esteem" also says exactly what it means. How much do you hold yourself in esteem? If you exchange your time for money, what is your time worth? And what do you base that on? In my master classes, independent business owners often make it clear that they'd like to charge higher rates, but they don't dare to increase their hourly fee. In most cases, this is driven by the fear that a customer might walk. If they did so, the customer would be indicating that they valued you less than you do. Do you want to work for or with someone like that? Of course, there's always a market mechanism that you can research and get a feel for, but who do you allow to determine your value?

What you think you're worth in terms of money is an automatic outgrowth of your self-esteem. That self-esteem is the cumulative result of your mindset and your different behavioral traits, including having self-esteem, a positive self-image, inner peace, grit, and charisma.

The opposite can have devastating effects. People with a lack of self-esteem and self-respect don't know their own unique qualities and don't make any effort to discover what those are. They often think poorly of themselves and constantly underestimate themselves. They behave dependently, often in a victim role. They don't take responsibility for their thoughts, deeds, and results. The people around them are often easily critical, and this easily throws people with low self-esteem off balance.

People who don't appreciate or respect themselves sufficiently repeatedly violate their own boundaries. It's hard for them to say no. They often think they're underpaid and undervalued but aren't quick to take targeted action to do something about it. They pay too little attention to their health and grooming. They don't have enough self-discipline to recognize and prevent (light) addictions—things like drinking too much, becoming significantly overweight, but also spending too much time on social media and letting themselves be guided by the opinions and judgments of those in their social environment. Troubled social relationships are also typical of people with a lack of self-esteem. A lack of self-confidence prevents them from independently achieving goals and growing as a human being.

What can you do to increase your self-esteem? You're doing that now by reading this book. You also have to put that knowledge into practice. Only by doing so can you build a powerful, positive personality. You can only replace a negative self-image with a positive one by being receptive, growing spiritually, and taking immediate, intensive, and lasting action.

Write down what you're good at. What are your strong attributes? And what qualities can you improve by working on them on a daily basis? Write down moments of success from the past and record your present moments of success every week. Always keep this overview on hand. Print it out and stick it on your bathroom mirror so you're reminded of your positive self every morning and evening. This is a form of auto-suggestion. If you combine it with writing down your affirmations (Step 5), you can constructively and structurally increase your feelings of self-esteem.

As you've read, Steps 1 and 2 define who you are and what you do. When you've mastered all the attributes of personal mastery and mindset, you'll be able to live your life the way you want. This forms the foundation for every success in your life. It's why they come before the other steps of the strategy. Is it then true that if you haven't yet mastered all the facets of personal mastery, you can't move on now? No, you can certainly move on to the next steps. But know that the more work you still need to do on yourself, the less easily you'll be able to take those next steps. Don't let this stop you, and, above all, keep moving forward.

But always keep working on your personal mastery and your mindset. I do, too, every day. It's a process of learning and continual self-improvement. That's what makes you a better person.

The Importance of Self-Discipline

Self-discipline is another pillar of personal mastery. It's the bridge between setting a goal and achieving it. Without discipline, even the best plans will fail. Discipline means doing what needs to be done, even when you don't feel like it. It means pushing through discomfort and staying committed to your goals.

As well-known author Jim Newman said, *"The secret of success is consistency of purpose."* Discipline is about consistency—doing the small, often mundane tasks that build up over time to create success. Whether it's waking up early to exercise, sticking to a budget, or working on a project when you'd rather relax, discipline is what keeps you moving forward.

Everyone can set goals, but not everyone achieves them because discipline is the key ingredient. It's easy to be excited about the goal-setting process, but the real challenge comes in the daily grind—waking up early, staying focused, and pushing through discomfort. That's where most people fall short.

The more disciplined you are, the more control you have over your life. When you commit to following through on your goals, something extraordinary happens: you begin to attract success, opportunities, and the right people into your life.

Self-discipline means making commitments to yourself and sticking to them—even when it's tough. It means doing things today that may not be enjoyable but will lead to a better future. These are the tasks that may not be fun but are crucial to your progress. Each time you keep a commitment to yourself, your self-confidence grows. Why? Because you're proving to yourself that you're reliable.

Imagine you have a friend who constantly fails to keep their promises. You were supposed to go to the gym together, but they didn't show up. They promised to take you out to dinner, but they forgot. They borrowed money from you and promised to pay it back, but they didn't. How would you feel about this friend? You'd probably start thinking that they don't value you. You'd likely lose trust in them.

This is also how your subconscious reacts when you make agreements with yourself but don't keep them. By doing so, you are sending a signal. Apparently, you are an unreliable person. This causes your self-confidence to decrease.

The same principle applies to how others treat you. If you allow people to break promises or disrespect you, it's a sign that your self-esteem is low. This is a form of *people-pleasing* behavior, where you allow others to dictate your life rather than setting and enforcing your own boundaries.

How to Train and Build Self-Discipline

There's a choice in life: the pain of discipline or the pain of regret. The pain of discipline is temporary, but the pain of regret can last a lifetime. That's the price you have to pay to achieve your goals.

The good news? Self-discipline can be trained. Start by deciding how you will spend your time. Establish regularity and create a schedule that reflects your priorities. But here's the crucial part: stick to the schedule even when you don't feel like it. For example, commit to doing at least one thing every day or every week that you've been putting off for too long. This could be anything—from a difficult conversation you need to have to paying a bill, cleaning your house, or finishing a project you started.

Stop procrastinating. Create a weekly (or daily) plan of tasks you want or need to complete. Then make a firm decision to get them done. Each time you keep these agreements with yourself, your self-confidence grows. Over time, this strengthens your ability to make even more powerful choices.

Self-discipline is not something you're born with; it's a skill you can develop through practice and conscious effort. It's about learning new, positive habits and unlearning negative ones—the ones that are holding you back. While it may not be easy, it is worth the effort. Self-discipline is the power that enables you to turn dreams into reality and reach your full potential. Discover this power within yourself and use it on your path to greatness. The question is, are you willing to put in the work? If you are, I can guarantee this: self-discipline is the key to unlocking your success.

The Journey of Personal Mastery

Personal mastery is not a destination; it's a journey that requires continual growth. Every day offers an opportunity to learn, improve, and refine your skills. The more you work on yourself, the easier it becomes to navigate the other steps of the 12-step strategy. As Jim Rohn said, "Success is something you attract by the person you become."

When you master yourself, you gain the power to shape your life in any way you choose. You become more resilient, more confident, and more capable of achieving your goals.

Personal mastery involves more than just mindset—it's about taking control of your health, emotions, time, relationships, finances, and career. It's about building self-esteem, practicing self-discipline, and mastering the art of communication. As you continue on this journey, you'll find that the more you work on yourself, the more you're able to accomplish in all areas of your life.

"A goal without a plan is just a wish."

– Antoine de Saint-Exupéry

Step 3: Set Clear and Concrete Goals

One of the greatest lessons I've learned is that goal setting is the starting point of all achievement. Goals act as the blueprint for your future, pulling you toward success, purpose, and fulfillment. Without goals, we drift. We get caught in the current of circumstances, allowing life to happen to us instead of taking control and designing the life we truly desire.

The first step in goal setting is clarity. You must know exactly what you want. This requires deep reflection—where do you want to be in 1 year, 5 years, or 10 years? Be specific. Saying "I want to be successful" isn't enough. What does success mean to you? Is it financial independence, strong relationships, or physical health? Write it down. A goal that isn't written down is just a wish. Clarity creates direction, and direction creates momentum.

Set Goals in Every Area of Life

Goals are about balance in all areas of life. Set goals for your *health*. You can't perform at your best if you're not physically capable. Set goals for your *relationships*. Life is better when you have meaningful connections with the people around you. Set goals for your *personal growth*, because the person you become in the pursuit of your goals is more important than the achievement itself.

There are four types of goals you can distinguish between when you start setting them:

1. **Personal development** – Who do you want to become? What behaviors or skills do you want to develop? What do you still want to learn? When you examine your behavior, what do you want, and what do you no longer want? Think of goals in the area of health or work, or at the mental, spiritual, relational, or social level. What concrete goals can you set to become the best version of yourself?

2. **Experiences** – What do you want to see and do? Travel or start a new hobby? Live abroad? Start and build your own company? Aim for meaningful experiences.

3. **Financial** – How much money do you want to make? Define specific financial goals and what lifestyle you want to achieve.

4. **Material** – What material things do you want? Whether it's a dream house, a car, a boat, a watch, or other luxury items, set realistic but inspiring material goals.

Brainstorm for 30 minutes, imagining anything is possible. Then, choose two main goals and two sub-goals to achieve within the next 12 months, plus one long-term dream. A *main goal* is something big—a significant achievement that will require time, focus, and dedication to complete. *Sub-goals* are smaller but still require effort and time. They may support your main goals or be independent achievements in their own right, contributing to your personal or professional growth.

Then write these goals down. Writing them down is crucial, in as much detail as you can, as if you've already accomplished all of it. As if you were looking at yourself in the future, when everything will already be as you would like it to be.

This is an effective way to set your personal goals. Once you've done that, it's important that you always picture your goal clearly and vividly before you and that you don't let go of that image until you've achieved it.

The Why Behind the Goal

It's not enough just to set goals. You must know *why* those goals matter to you. The "why" gives you power.

My goal was to become a millionaire, a wizard, a DJ, and a world sailor. And then a writer and speaker. But those are just words. Behind every goal lies a reason, a "why." At its root, that reason is borne of necessity or boundless desire.

The goals you set may inspire you, but when the journey gets tough—and believe me, it will get tough—it's your "why" that will keep you moving. It's easy to quit when you don't have a compelling reason to keep going.

So, when you set a goal, ask yourself, *Why do I want to achieve this? What will it mean to me, my family, my future? How will it improve my life?* Get emotionally involved with your goals. The deeper your connection to your "why," the more determined you'll be to achieve it.

Don't be afraid to dream big. If you're going to set a goal, make it worth your while. Don't settle for mediocrity. But—and here's the balance—you also need to understand that success is achieved one step at a time. You don't conquer the highest mountain in one leap; you do it one base camp at a time. Set big goals but start small.

If you have a big end goal, you'll need to build in smaller, intermediate goals. Having a step-by-step plan in which you break down the path to your goal makes the process more manageable and your goal easier to reach. You can't climb a whole flight of stairs in a single step, but you can do it step-by-step, the same way the highest peaks are scaled.

Every day, you should be taking small actions that move you closer to your goal. You don't need to achieve everything at once, but you do need to be making progress *every single day.*

Set a deadline, but be sure to give yourself enough time. That creates a sense of peace and prevents stress. It's also important to realize that your life plan doesn't have to be pre-programmed from one minute to the next. Know where you want to go, but don't panic if you temporarily stray from your path or take a timeout. Don't focus blindly on the route. We all have moments when we no longer know what to do or in which direction we want our lives to go. It's okay in those moments to take your foot off the gas and to make sure you first get a thorough overview of your situation again by asking good questions. A stretch of just doing nothing can sometimes do no harm either. Moments of rest are really important for the quality of your life. From a place of calm, you generally make wiser choices.

To set your internal compass, you first need to know exactly where you want to go. How you'll get there doesn't matter before you set out, but you do need to know where you want to end up. You never know in advance what will come up along the way, which means you'll have to deal with those things as you go in order to reach your goal. The bigger your goal, the less likely you are to lose sight of it if a minor problem or setback comes between you. It's essential that your goal, the destination, is perfectly clear. You have to be able to see it before you. Again, it comes down to visualization and imagination. Begin with the end in mind.

Your goal may be to become financially independent or travel the world. To find the love of your life or buy your dream house. It could be anything. But a goal doesn't always have to be so big. Losing 10 pounds is a concrete goal. So is learning to speak a language, getting a good grade on a test, passing your driving test, reading for 15 minutes every day, or taking an hour each day for yourself.

With everything I tell you in this book, my objective is to help you achieve your goals so you can start living your best life, whatever "your best life" may mean to you. Where do you want to go? Who do you want to be? What do you want to have? What do you want to do? What do you want to accomplish? In short: What's your destination?

Goals: Realistic or Not

I don't think you need to set "realistic" goals, but you do need to be realistic about where you are at the moment: mentally, physically, financially, emotionally, and in terms of knowledge and preparation. Thinking big is fine, but start small. Running a marathon (a good metaphor for the many goals you want to achieve) within a week without training for it is virtually impossible, not to mention irresponsible. You first need to train and prepare properly for months. You can learn to play the piano beautifully, only you won't get to that point in a week or even a few months. It takes long-term practice, discipline, and dedication.

For years, my dream was to live on a boat and take sailing trips to sunny locales on clear blue waters. That idea came about when I was six years old and my father took me out on a network of lakes in a small, rented boat. It took 30 years for me to make that dream come true. I had to set up companies, work extremely hard for years, and overcome a lot of setbacks before I finally gained financial independence. But it was all worth it. You become great by growing, learning, and improving yourself a little bit every day.

I regularly notice that people have trouble being realistic about the time frame in which they want to achieve a particular goal. There's this lack of patience. People are often too eager, or even too greedy, which should not be confused with enthusiasm and drive. They often overestimate what's possible within a year and underestimate what's achievable within three to five years. In five years, your life may look completely different if you change your course now. It's up to you where you choose to go. What your life will be like in five years is the result of your thinking, your behavior, your mentality, the choices you make, and the actions you take today.

I Like a Million Things

I often hear that people find it difficult to set goals. "I like so many things," someone will say. "I can think of a thousand goals." That's not true. If it were, it would be simple: choose one or two, draw up a plan, carry it out, and achieve your goal. Not being able to choose means that you don't find any goal really worthwhile, so then there's a lack of clarity and no specific desire.

When I keep asking questions to get to the bottom of things, these millions of things often turn out to be nothing more than a collection of vague wishes. "I'd like to be rich too." "I'd like to write a book about my life." "I'd like to take a trip around the world." "Maybe I should do something with my talent." "People often tell me I'm a good cook—maybe I should start a restaurant." This doesn't attest to knowing what you really want. Determining a goal means you choose and take action. What kind of restaurant? What does it look like? What kind of cuisine? Make your plan, rent a space, set up the restaurant, and start cooking. No money is no excuse. If you really want something, you'll be inventive enough and find a way. Don't let your excuses be bigger than your dreams. Take charge of your own life.

"There's always a reason not to do it," said a seasoned sailor and good friend, when he sailed with me years ago. He told me how many people who had plans to sail around the earth asked him for advice. Most of them never set sail. "Afraid they have too little money or that they'll no longer find a job when they get back. They're afraid that they aren't properly prepared; there are so many more jobs to be done on the boat first. It's not the right boat. Then it's the kids, so they wait. After that, their parents are at an age that it wouldn't be prudent to leave, so they put it off again. And in the end, they reach an age where they think they're too old or can't take on the physical challenge any longer." Tomorrow never comes.

I started living my big dream when I was 40, when I pulled up anchor and sailed off. Five summers and many beautiful destinations later, I changed course. After many thousands of miles on the Mediterranean, I discovered a reason not to continue on around the world. A new mission had appeared on my path, a new goal. The irresistible desire to travel was no longer there; things were fine the way they were. And I thought of my friend's words: "There's always a reason to not do something." There's also always a reason to do something.

Goals give you direction and something to hold on to. They keep you from drifting aimlessly. Build in regular check-ins to evaluate your progress, to determine where you stand and how far you are from your final goal.

Choosing and achieving your goals means you have to set priorities. You could consider making a list of goals every week, what you want to have done or accomplished by the end of that week. When it comes to bigger goals, I advise you to choose a maximum of four per year. It'll already be challenging enough to manage your time and attention in a way that enables you to actually achieve these goals. The maxim is simple: the bigger the goal, the more time and attention it will require.

Goal setting isn't a one-time event. You must continually review and adjust your goals as you go. Life is dynamic. Things change. Circumstances shift. But here's the beauty of goal setting: it gives you direction, but it doesn't trap you. If you need to adjust your course, that's okay. Just don't give up on the destination.

Take time to review your progress regularly. Are you on track? Are your actions aligned with your goals? What needs to change? Success is a constant process of small corrections, like a pilot adjusting their course to reach the destination. Stay flexible but focused.

Goal setting is the foundation of a life well-lived. It bridges the gap between where you are and where you want to be. Don't leave your future to chance. Success doesn't happen by accident—it happens by design. Set clear, specific, and meaningful goals. Create a plan and go after them with everything you've got. The future is yours if you're willing to go after it!

> *"First believe, then you will see.*
> *That is my mantra."*
>
> **– Michael Pilarczyk**

Step 4: Visualize the End Result

Visualization is one of the most powerful tools you have to let your subconscious work alongside you in achieving your goals and dreams. You have to *see* things in your mind's eye as if they are already happening. It's like programming yourself to succeed.

Albert Einstein once said, *"Imagination is more important than knowledge,"* and there's a deep truth to that. Charles Garfield, an American psychologist and professor at the University of California at San Francisco, explored this concept extensively in his 1987 bestseller *Peak Performers*. He conducted groundbreaking research into people who had achieved remarkable success in their fields, and one of his key findings was that visualization plays a huge role in peak performance.

Garfield saw firsthand how astronauts at NASA trained by rehearsing their missions in simulators, over and over again, before ever setting foot in space. This repeated practice of mental preparation led him to explore the concept of self-programming through visualization further. His research revealed a common trait among top performers—whether athletes, artists, politicians, or business leaders—they all excel at visualizing their end goals. They don't just think about success; they see it, feel it, and experience it before taking any physical action. They start with the end in mind, exactly as Stephen Covey describes in *The 7 Habits of Highly Effective People*.

The power of visualization is the power of imagination. Napoleon Hill understood this well and wrote extensively about it in *Think and Grow Rich*. Through his research on hundreds of successful people at the turn of the twentieth century, Hill discovered that imagination was a key factor in their achievements. It's no coincidence that imagination is essential for inventors and visionaries. Think about the great minds behind life-changing inventions—electricity, the telephone, the internet—these innovations started in someone's mind long before they became reality. Look around you: almost everything you see was once just an idea. If you can imagine it, you can create it.

Visualizing is simply the practice of clearly imagining the end result of what you want to achieve. You need to *see* and *feel* that outcome, as if it's already happening. When you make your visualization vivid and realistic, it becomes a form of mental rehearsal. It's no coincidence that successful artists, athletes, and business leaders regularly use visualization and auto-suggestion to sharpen their focus and reinforce their goals.

Without even realizing it at the time, I visualized myself as a DJ on national radio long before it happened. In my thoughts, I was already there, in the studio, presenting programs. I could feel the energy of the place. Years later, I found myself sailing on clear, blue waters—another visualization turned reality. As a boy, I would fill my room with posters of sailboats, tropical islands, and endless blue seas. I could see it, feel it, and hear the sounds of the waves and the wind. Those images were so vivid in my mind that they became a part of me.

When I decided to find a home in Ibiza, I knew exactly what I wanted. I created a list: a house with a sun deck, peaceful surroundings, no more than 20 minutes from civilization, and with a fast, reliable internet connection. Most importantly, it had to be on the water, where I could see and hear the sea from the house. Every day, I visualized that home. I saw myself walking through the house, gazing out at the water, feeling the sea breeze.

It wasn't long before that exact vision became my reality. Not by itself, of course. But we found the house as Cindy and I had visualized it, partly because we knew exactly what we were looking for.

"Live within when you're without," Dan Peña taught me years ago. See the life you want to live is already happening in your thoughts. Feel it, smell it, experience it. That's also the reason he holds his Quantum Leap Advantage seminars at his castle in Scotland—he immerses people in a world of luxury and success so they can begin to see themselves living that life.

If you're dreaming of a new car, for example, go to the dealership and take a test drive. Sit in the exact model you want. Let yourself *feel* like it's already yours. The more you experience that feeling, the more real it becomes.

Sometimes, it's not so easy to make your goals tangible, and that's when imagination becomes your greatest tool. To make what you're imagining as visual as possible, put together a vision board: a clear collage of your goal or a visual representation of what you want your life to look like. Look at it every day. Let it condition your subconscious mind. You are the architect of your life, and your vision board is your blueprint. But remember, while your life is largely self-designed, it won't always go exactly as planned. Accept that reality and make peace with it.

Different Approaches to Visualization

There are many ways to incorporate visualization into your life. One simple method is to visualize each morning, as a kind of rehearsal for the day ahead. Imagine how you want your day to unfold—what you want to accomplish, how you want to feel, and the success you aim to achieve.

You can also use visualization for long-term goals. Focus on your dream, your ultimate goal. Give it your full attention.

When you focus on one goal at a time during visualization, other helpful images often come to you naturally, guiding you along the way. Take your time with this. Visualize what your best life looks like.

It's important to note that visualizations are especially effective when you're in a state of deep inner peace. Make sure you're in a positive state of being. This may sound somewhat elusive, but it's not: go to the vibrations of love, trust, and gratitude. Then you'll start to "vibrate" at the right energy frequency and be able to connect with your subconscious and Cosmic Intelligence. If you take time in this meditative state of being, images will appear, sometimes very vague, sometimes crystal clear.

Your Thoughts Create Your Reality

Visualization is closely tied to the principle of reaping what you sow. When you operate from a place of fear, insecurity, or disbelief, you send the wrong signals to your subconscious and the universe, which often leads to unwanted results. The energy you put out is the frequency you live in—it's the foundation of the reality you create.

Before you start visualizing, seek out silence. Calm your mind and body. Meditation can help with this. You might focus on a specific goal and make it as vivid as possible. Or you might choose to clear your mind and allow images to come to you naturally. You'll know you're in the right state when you're no longer actively thinking, but simply observing the images and feelings that come through. Don't interrupt the flow with rational thoughts—just let it happen.

As long as your mind is restless, it will be difficult to tune into the right frequency. The key is to let go and allow the right energy, based on trust, love, and gratitude, to guide you. The more you practice, the better you'll get. When you're in the right state, you'll know it. But the moment you consciously try to analyze what's happening, you'll break the flow.

In summary, visualization is all about imagination. Make sure you're in a relaxed, positive state, and let your thoughts flow freely. Take your time. First, connect with feelings of love, trust, and gratitude. You can visualize with your eyes open or closed—it doesn't matter. The important thing is to see your goals as if they're already happening right now. It's not about imagining the future but living the experience in your mind in the present moment. Begin with the end in mind, and remember, as Einstein said, *imagination is more important than knowledge*.

Begin With the End in Mind

When I was writing *Dancing in Heaven*, I did something that might seem a little unusual. I created a homemade book cover that featured the words "100,000 copies sold" along with a picture of me on it, and I put it on my MacBook. Why? Because every time I opened my computer, I wanted to see that image. I wanted my subconscious to start believing it was real. The more I saw that visualized outcome, the more I became convinced—both consciously and unconsciously—that my goal was possible.

After the writing was finished, I didn't stop there. I began imagining what it would be like to walk into a bookstore and see stacks of blue books with my name on the cover. In my mind's eye, I strolled through the aisles, spotted my book on the shelves, and felt the excitement of knowing that people would soon be reading it. This image wasn't just a fleeting thought—it became a part of my daily routine. And sure enough, just a few months later, that visualization became a reality.

But here's the thing: I didn't know how to write a novel when I first started, and I had no experience in the publishing world.

That didn't stop me. I was determined to see my goal through. I followed a novel-writing course at The Amsterdam School for Writers, I scoured the internet for everything I could learn about writing and publishing, and I bought and studied nearly every book on the topic. I had a clear vision: I wanted my book to reach 100,000 readers and make it onto the top-10 bestseller list.

While I was working on my novel, I didn't just sit back and wait for things to fall into place. I did my homework. I asked people around me how often they read books and when they were most likely to pick up a novel. Their answers were telling: they rarely read, and when they did, it was usually during the summer break.

It was March 2014, and after three years of hard work, my story was finally finished. But my book wasn't yet on the shelves, and summer—the prime time for readers—was fast approaching. I needed *Dancing in Heaven* to be in stores by May, but my experienced editor, Mr. B., warned me that finding a publisher and getting the book out by then was nearly impossible.

Still, I didn't let that discourage me. I contacted several publishers, and while some showed interest, nothing concrete came of it. Then one day, I met with a third-party publisher who agreed to hear me out. I told her I wanted 10,000 copies of my book in stores by the end of May, and I asked what kind of investment her publishing house would make in the project. Her answer? "Pretty much nothing." That wasn't the response I'd hoped for. I proposed to finance the first print run and the marketing spend myself, but she advised me against it. During our pleasant conversation, I'd briefly mentioned my entrepreneurial experience to her, after which she suggested, "Why don't you publish it yourself?"

That was the turning point. I had never considered self-publishing, but it suddenly felt like the perfect solution. I gratefully accepted her advice, despite the fact that everyone around me tried to discourage me from starting my own publishing company. I was warned that it would be risky, and that self-publishing wasn't a wise move for someone without experience. But I trusted the process, just as Dan Peña's strategy had taught me: collaborate with someone who has a strong track record to gain credibility.

By chance—or maybe by design—I crossed paths with Elise de Bres, an experienced publisher. She was exactly the partner I needed. Together, we assembled a dream team, including a designer and a proofreader, to make my vision a reality. But we still faced one big question: How do we get my book into stores?

Elise introduced me to two industry veterans with strong contacts in the book trade, and together, we started brainstorming creative marketing ideas. One of the most innovative strategies we came up with was to distribute the first 500 copies of *Dancing in Heaven* for free to passengers on trains. I reached out to the National Railways with this proposal, but they declined, worried that it might cause chaos on the platforms.

After three rejections, I wasn't ready to give up. I offered to create a special edition of the book with "Compliments of the National Railways" on the cover. This time, they were intrigued.

Meanwhile, we had another challenge: getting the media interested. At first, magazines and newspapers didn't seem particularly eager to cover the book. That's when Cindy, our marketing expert, suggested promoting *Dancing in Heaven* on Facebook. To be honest, I wasn't sure how effective social media would be, but Cindy was confident. Her idea was to record well-known people reading excerpts from the book aloud and post the videos online.

There was just one problem: I wasn't exactly well-connected. After years of sailing around the world, I hadn't kept up with many of my contacts. I sent emails to dozens of people, many of which went unanswered. But eventually, a few said yes, and we were able to put the videos together.

Then one day, I remembered that a journalist I knew was a Facebook friend. I reached out, and the next day he called to ask if I'd be interested in sharing my feature story with a national newspaper. That article ended up being a game-changer for the book's promotion, and I'll always be grateful for his help.

Looking back, the journey of *Dancing in Heaven* is a perfect example of the strategy I'm teaching you. I followed the 12 steps as I describe them here. Some luck may have come my way here and there, but it was a path I'd consciously chosen to walk.

I had a clear end goal in mind, I did my research, I gathered a dream team, and I put together a strategic plan. I stayed focused and did everything I could to make my vision a success. But most importantly, I visualized the outcome from the very beginning.

By the end of 2014, *Dancing in Heaven* had achieved everything I'd visualized. It landed in the top 10 bestselling novels of the year, with over 100,000 copies sold. More than just a dream, my visualization had become my reality.

So, here's what you need to remember: Start with the end in mind. Visualize your dream clearly, see the final result in your mind's eye, and take deliberate steps to make it happen. If you can imagine it, you can achieve it.

Step 5: Write Down Your Affirmations

Visualization is a crucial part of the process, but let's be clear: the law of attraction and creation only works when you work on it. You need a concrete plan backed by action. It's not enough to send a wish into the universe and then sit back and relax. That's just a fairy tale.

To manifest your goals and achieve success, you must take action. One way to reinforce your visualization is through affirmations. These are positive statements that you write down and repeat regularly. The power lies in repetition. By repeating an affirmation hundreds, or even thousands, of times, you program it into your subconscious until it becomes a belief you truly embody.

Write down your affirmations as if you've already achieved your goal. Use the present tense, and make them personal, positive, and filled with emotion. Keep them short, to preserve the essence and feeling. Be specific—vague affirmations can lead to unintended outcomes.

For example, avoid saying, "I want to do fun things," or "I'm going to earn a lot of money," or "I want to feel happy." Your subconscious can't work with such imprecise intentions. Instead, write affirmations like, "I enjoy every moment of my fulfilling life," or "I am financially abundant," or "I am filled with happiness and gratitude." These are clear, emotionally charged, and direct.

Why Do Affirmations Work?

Faith is the most powerful alchemist of the mind. When a thought is combined with emotion, something magical happens. An affirmation is a positive, emotionally charged thought about your future self, spoken as if it's happening now. Repeating this thought enough transforms it into a belief and, eventually, a deep conviction. Your subconscious picks up the frequency and sends that signal to the universe—or as I call it, Cosmic Intelligence. When that happens, coincidences, opportunities, and what we might call "luck" begin to appear, moving you closer to your vision. What you imagine, you become.

Faith and conviction are developed through auto-suggestion—repeating instructions to your subconscious mind. Your subconscious acts like a memory bank, storing everything you see and hear—both positive and negative—and influencing your behavior.

Your subconscious doesn't distinguish between reality and imagination; it accepts vivid images as real. While you can't control it directly, you can influence it through the information you expose yourself to. That happens automatically, through everything you see and hear, every moment of your life. News stories, social media, the opinions of others, what others say to you. Whether that information is correct or not, you turn it into what you want to believe in your brain because of your conditioning. By feeding your subconscious with positive, emotionally charged thoughts, you reprogram it on an energetic level, influencing your reality. That's why affirmations are so powerful.

Faith is the force behind every miracle and mystery. It transforms thought vibrations into spiritual signals and is the starting point of success. When you combine faith with emotion, you unlock a connection that brings your desires closer to reality.

You can plant any thought or goal into your subconscious by saying it out loud repeatedly. Your dominant thoughts—the ones that shape your behavior—ultimately shape your reality. Repeated affirmations strengthen your self-worth, confidence, and belief in your ability to achieve anything you set your mind to.

If you can't imagine something is possible, it never will be. Affirmations, visualization, and auto-suggestion are tools that allow you to rewire your brain for success. They are most effective when practiced daily, in a calm and peaceful state of mind. The more often you read and repeat them, the more deeply they become ingrained in your subconscious, eventually shaping your reality.

The Power of Writing Things Down

Writing down your affirmations is essential. The physical act of writing—pen to paper, not typing on your laptop or into your phone—imprints itself in your cells, heart, brain, and subconscious. Like breathing exercises that connect body and mind, writing connects your thoughts and dreams, making them tangible.

Some doubt the power of affirmations, but that often comes from not understanding how the brain works. Neural networks—the pathways that shape your habits—are built through repetition. Auto-suggestion bridges your conscious thoughts and your subconscious mind. Through consistent visualization and affirmations, you develop new thought patterns that guide you toward success.

Daily Affirmations

Your dominant thoughts shape your reality. That's why I advise you to dedicate 10 minutes every day to focusing on the person you want to become and the life you want to live. Visualize the life you desire, and see yourself achieving your goals. Believe in your ability to make it all happen.

When you repeat your affirmations with total focus and genuine emotion, they become powerful. Below are some examples you can use to create your own affirmations. Starting with "I am grateful..." creates strong, positive vibrations, and many of my own affirmations begin this way:

- I am grateful for this day.
- I am grateful for who I am.
- I am grateful for the opportunities that come my way.
- I am happy and grateful to be living my best life.
- I deserve to live a healthy, rich, and happy life.
- I trust that I am guided by higher powers.
- I have the courage to do what's right.
- I feel love in myself and share that love with others.
- I live in a place of trust and abundance.
- I am fully capable of achieving anything I set my mind to.
- I am blessed with my talents and the opportunities life offers me.

- I make an effort to improve myself every day.
- I have a lot of self-confidence.
- I live from a place of trust.
- I am invincible.
- I am living my best life, and for that I am grateful.
- My life is filled with blessings, and I am grateful.

Feel It, See It, Live It

This is particularly important: keep in mind that if you read your affirmations (out loud or in silence) but don't truly believe them, they won't work. Affirmations only work when they're backed by emotion and conviction. You have to really mean it. You have to believe it. Feel it, see it, live it. Your subconscious only responds to thoughts that carry strong emotional energy. Empty words won't affect it.

Putting this process into practice can be challenging, especially at first. So be patient. Write down a few affirmations—don't overcomplicate it—and focus on putting your subconscious to work for you. Read your affirmations every morning and evening until they're etched into your memory. Don't write an entire book of affirmations at once. Focus on a handful that really resonate with you. Personally, I find it powerful to repeat one affirmation multiple times in a row, allowing it to sink deeper into my consciousness.

At first, writing down your affirmations and saying them out loud might seem unnecessary. That's exactly what I thought when I first read *Think and Grow Rich*. But once I began consistently writing down my affirmations and saying them daily—repeatedly, both out loud and in my mind—the results started to appear. The skeptical part of my mind faded away, replaced by a growing faith. And then, faith transformed into rock-solid conviction. That's when you know it's working. That's when you'll be able to say, with certainty: "I am the master of my fate. I am the captain of my soul."

> *"A good coach can change a game.*
> *A great coach can change a life."*
>
> **– John Wooden**

Step 6: Have Role Models

Success leaves clues, and one of the golden rules is to follow the example of those who have achieved what you aim to accomplish. It's like using a cookbook—when you want to create something, you find a recipe and follow it. The same goes for success. Find role models in your chosen field or people who inspire you. Study, copy, and emulate them. But always remember to put enough of *yourself* into it; it's about learning from others, not becoming a carbon copy.

If you want to be successful, study successful people. If you want to be happy, study happy people. If you want to accumulate wealth, learn from those who have done so. Follow the model.

This is an important step. If you want to master something— whether it's business, entrepreneurship, finance, communication, meditation, cooking, writing, marketing, relationships, health, sports, music, psychology, or mindset—you need a role model. Find someone who is already where you want to be. Study their behavior, their mindset, and their habits. Read every interview, watch every video, dive into any book or documentary that explores their life and achievements.

Your role models don't have to be world-famous. They can be someone in your community or a person in your field who's had significant success. But do your homework—be sure your role models are genuine. Especially in today's world, where social media can create the illusion of success, it's important to dig deeper into their actual accomplishments. Not everything is as it seems online.

Ask yourself these essential questions when choosing your role models: "Where did they come from?" "How did they start?" "What path did they take?" "What setbacks did they face?" "Who were their mentors?" "What makes them unique?" "What can I learn from them?"

We all look up to role models, both consciously and unconsciously—whether it's our parents, friends, experts, teachers, or even heroes. Often, these are people we interact with in everyday life. Because of this, we can quickly become the average of the people we surround ourselves with. Their influence—whether positive or negative—rubs off on us more than we realize. This is why you have to be careful not to end up with the wrong role models, as that can lead to negative thinking or behavior.

Choose your role models carefully. Be mindful of the behaviors and mindsets you adopt. Who are the people you look up to? What do they do? How do they think? How did they become successful? What makes them stand out? Do your research.

Almost all successful people—whether in business, sports, or the arts—have had role models who inspired them.

Take LeBron James, for example. Growing up, he looked up to basketball greats like Michael Jordan and Magic Johnson, studying their games and using their achievements as a roadmap for his own success.

Steve Jobs was heavily influenced by innovators like Edwin Land, the inventor of the Polaroid camera, and also by Robert Friedland, a spiritual leader and entrepreneur, who introduced Jobs to the idea of thinking differently.

Serena Williams has often cited her older sister Venus as one of her biggest inspirations. Growing up together, Venus paved the way in the tennis world, and her hard work and success motivated Serena to push herself even further.

In politics, we see the influence of role models. Barack Obama often cited figures like Martin Luther King Jr. and Nelson Mandela as inspirations for his leadership. These are just a few examples of people who have reached extraordinary heights by following the path laid out by their role models.

Personally, I've always had role models, and they've shaped the course of my life. It started with my uncle John, whose luxury lifestyle lit the path for my own ambitions. When I dreamed of being on the radio, my hero was MTV's Adam Curry, with his legendary radio and TV shows. I also studied the legendary *Scott & Todd in the Morning* on WPLJ RADIO in New York. Back then, the internet wasn't around, so I had to find cassette tapes of these shows, which I played over and over until I could mimic every word—or until the tapes wore out.

Before I became a TV host, David Letterman was my inspiration. I studied hundreds of his *Late Show* episodes, not because I wanted to be a late-night host, but because I admired his performance style and his ability to engage an audience. Even now, I love watching the interviews he does on Netflix.

The key is not to become a copy of your role model. Think of them as study material—take the qualities and behaviors that resonate with you, and then add your own unique spin. Also, don't limit yourself to one role model; learn from several people who excel in different areas.

When I started my sailing adventures, ocean sailor Henk de Velde was my role model. Dan Peña taught me to embrace the mindset of unlimited possibilities. His lessons empowered me to take bold steps into the business world with confidence. In personal development, Tony Robbins and Jim Rohn have been two of the most influential figures. Their lessons helped me shift my mindset to reach higher levels of success. In my current work,

I also draw inspiration from spiritual teachers like Deepak Chopra, Rajshree Patel, and my life coach, Egon Massink.

Role models don't always have to be contemporary. I still learn from the wisdom of past greats like Wayne Dyer, Bob Proctor, and Alan Watts. Fortunately, their knowledge lives on in books, audio, and video, which I pass on to you in my own way.

So, who are *your* role models? Find people who inspire you, and study their journey. Follow the example of those who are already where you want to be. Success leaves clues—learn from them.

Step 7: Research Before You Begin

"The more you investigate, the less you have to invest" is one of Dan Peña's golden rules. In other words, the better your research, the less time, money, and effort you'll need to invest later. The more prepared you are, the more you'll understand what you're doing, increasing your chances of success and reducing unnecessary stress.

Think of a time you had to take a test. If you studied well, you might have felt a little nervous, but you were confident because you knew the material. On the other hand, if you crammed the night before and realized you didn't fully understand what was being tested, stress probably took over. Good preparation is half the work. Approach your research with curiosity.

Avoid saying things like:

- "It won't work out."
- "It's impossible."
- "I don't know the right people."
- "The risk is too great."
- "I don't believe in that."
- "How am I supposed to get this done?"

These kinds of thoughts hold you back. Don't focus too much on all the things that can go wrong. People who do—and there are many of them—have little faith in their abilities and primarily see the world through a negative lens. Don't focus on the problem, focus on the solution!

It is wise, however, to assess risks early on. But do it purposefully and systematically, not obsessively. Create a list of relevant questions and answer them. Consider doing a SWOT analysis—assessing the Strengths, Weaknesses, Opportunities, and Threats of your plan. Ask yourself, "What could go wrong?" "What's the worst that could happen?" and think about ways to minimize those risks.

Consult people who can give you valuable feedback on your idea. Friends and family aren't usually experts. You can ask them for their opinions, but they can only respond from their points of view, and that's probably more likely to confuse you than be of value. Ask specialists for advice. Ask the right people good questions. After all, if you're building a house, you wouldn't ask a dentist for advice, even if they're the best at what they do.

Also, ask yourself: "Who are my competitors?" "How do they succeed?" Study them thoroughly. You need to understand the landscape you're entering and what the rules of the game are. Then, mirror them.

> *"Our goals can only be reached through a plan, in which we must fervently believe, and upon which we must vigorously act. There is no other route to success."*
> **– Pablo Picasso**

As I've said before: if you want to be successful, study successful people. If you want to be happy, study happy people. If you want to be wealthy, study wealthy people. And if you want to develop spiritually, study spiritual books, take courses, and learn from spiritual teachers.

Whatever areas you want to grow in, continuous learning and doing your homework is essential. But don't let research become an excuse for procrastination. See Step 10—do your research, but start as soon as possible, even if you don't feel fully ready.

Step 8: Create a Strategic Plan

Start by drawing up a clear strategic plan based on your idea and research. Ask yourself: *"Who and what do I need to make this idea a success?"* These are essential questions. Equally important is defining what success looks like. Make your goals measurable—without clear metrics, it's impossible to track progress or know how close you are to achieving your objectives.

You don't need an overly detailed business plan with endless spreadsheets at the beginning. The key is simplicity. If the essence of your plan isn't clear within a few sentences, it's likely too complex. And if you can't explain your idea concisely to others, it means either you don't fully understand it, or the concept is unnecessarily complicated. Simplicity is crucial—not only to keep things manageable but to ensure that you can explain it convincingly.

How do you get from where you are to where you want to be? Start with Step 1, and keep moving forward. With each step, the path becomes clearer, and a roadmap will begin to take shape.

The plan is especially important for you, so you know what you are going to do. At this stage, you don't need to work out every financial detail. Instead, focus on having concise, realistic numbers to support your plan. You'll have the opportunity to track and update key financial figures as you go. If you need financing from the start, you'll need a well-founded financial and strategic plan, but be prepared—these plans often deviate from reality once you begin implementation.

Put your step-by-step plan on paper with passion. But be willing to alter your course. Because from the moment you start executing the plan, you will have to make adjustments as a result of what you encounter. No matter how thorough your research or how solid your plan, unexpected setbacks will happen. Never underestimate how much things can change.

Step 9: Create Your Dream Team

Whatever you do, you can never achieve it alone. Success is always a collaborative effort. Top athletes have trainers and coaches. Musicians rely on songwriters, producers, and managers. Writers need editors and publishers. Even in business, success depends on having a strong team—much like a good marriage where partners complement each other.

At home, you have one kind of team; at work, you need another. Surround yourself with the right people. When you're starting a business, it's crucial to bring in individuals with a proven track record—those who have experience and have achieved success. These are the people who can help you get to where you want to be.

An important question to ask yourself is "Who do I need to do what?" First you need to know who's missing from your team. Why do you need someone else to support you? A specialist to do what? If you create clarity on what kind of person you need, then you can start searching for that additional talent.

When I talk about dream teams, the question always comes up: Where do you find these people, and why would they partner with you? Again, first be very clear about who you need for what. Then work out where to find those kinds of people. Preferably, know very specifically who, so identify their names and phone numbers or email addresses. The answer to the second question is: What do you have to offer? What's your added value? Other people will almost never commit to you simply out of charity, especially not if they're specialists, people with packed schedules who aren't sitting around waiting for you. So how do you interest those people? Make sure you have something to offer that's interesting enough for them. There has to be a mutual interest. The other person must also benefit. If you're not creative enough for this and don't have enough to offer, it'll probably be difficult to assemble a team around you.

Here's a personal example of a dream team. On December 11, 1992, I had the honor of spinning the very first record on Radio 538. At the time of its founding, we put together a radio dream team. To round out that team, the founder had clever business partners, specialists in their field. What started out as an idea of the founder soon came to life in the minds of the entire team. We became the most-listened station thanks to unstoppable drive and perseverance of all who worked there. The radio station was not just a job; it was our life, our everything. The collective desire to become the most popular radio station became a reality a few years later. Originating from one man's idea, our passion grew into a company worth more than $200 million.

During my first seminar week at Guthrie Castle, I learned the principle of the dream team. I was 29 years old at the time. In line with Dan Peña's QLA method, I assembled a team to start my first media company, choosing them both for their knowledge and for the credibility they would bring. I needed professionals who had earned their spurs and who could add something I didn't have: business experience in taking over companies and arranging financing in the tens of millions.

Of course, a good question to ask yourself is "Why would someone like this want to be of service to me?" If you have an idea in mind, you may now also be wondering how you can put such a team of top performers in place around you. Most entrepreneurs, top managers, and successful people manage their time carefully and spend it mainly on their own activities, so you'll really have to have something to offer that is of interest to others. There has to be a common interest, a shared stake. If you can't in any way provide added value or something interesting, others won't be willing to free up time to pay attention to you.

When I started my first media company, my added value was that I had valuable contacts in the media world, had my fame, was able to put together a team of creative and passionate employees, had developed and sold a number of TV show formats, and had devised a strategic plan to allow me to create a very valuable company in a short time. These things helped me capture the interest of investors.

It's all about being able to tell a convincing story so you can sell yourself and your dream. This is only possible if you do it with passion and if you believe in yourself a thousand percent. That belief in yourself is your greatest power. From there, it comes down to your communication skills, your personality, and your positive mental attitude.

Besides putting together your business dream team, you need to find a key player for your personal team—a coach. Successful people have coaches. Athletes are an obvious example of this. Even if they're among the world's best, every top athlete has a coach. Many entrepreneurs also get guidance or advice from older, more experienced entrepreneurs or from people who are "retired."

Everyone needs a coach or a mentor, someone who can hold a mirror up to them and tell them from experience what they're doing right and wrong. A coach is a trusted adviser with whom you can discuss everything and who gets more out of you than you ever thought possible.

In the past 35 years, I've met a lot of sensible and successful people from whom I've learned a great deal. Generally speaking, older people have a great deal of knowledge, life experience, and valuable wisdom, and they're often willing to share that. Make grateful use of it.

> *"You don't have to be great to get started,*
> *but you have to get started to be great."*

> **– Zig Ziglar**

Step 10: Move Before You're Ready

Simply starting might sound too basic to deserve its own step, yet here it is—because too many people never start, or they wait too long. Don't wait for the perfect plan. Waiting for "the right moment" is often an illusion. Don't wait for anything. "One day leads to a town called nowhere."

Opportunities don't wait for you; they come and go. Be aware of this. Stay alert and seize them when they come. Do enough research to understand your next steps, but start executing your plan as soon as possible. This is what I call "Move before you're ready." It's better to have a good plan you can start on today than to wait for a perfect plan that may never come. Perfect plans don't exist.

I once knew someone who spent years bombarding me with ideas. A few of them had real potential and, in my view, could have been highly successful. But as a university-educated scholar, he kept researching and waiting—for the perfect plan, for the right timing, for a collaboration that never materialized, or for a shortcut to success.

As a simple entrepreneur, I've learned that success often lies in simplicity. The mountain gets climbed because you start moving. Scholars tend to stand at the base, trying to find a quicker way to the top by using their intelligence. But when I reach the summit and look down, I often see them still at the bottom, still overthinking their approach.

Every time you climb a new mountain, you have to start at the bottom. Whatever your reputation, however good you are, and however high the mountain is—none of those matters. You have to start at the bottom, and you only get closer to the top by moving and continuing to move.

People often tell me, "I have no clue where to start!" This usually means they don't have a clear destination. If things aren't concrete, it's tough to begin. But if you know what you want or, even better, if you have a plan, keep it simple. Start at the beginning—or rather, start with the end in mind. When you know where you want to go, you can chart your course. Don't get caught up in designing business cards, logos, or building websites. Take action as soon as possible, and start testing your ideas in the real world.

When we started with the Meditation Moments app, we also applied the principle of "Move before you're ready." I had always led meditations at our live events, and we saw their impact on the attendees. After one event, two young tech experts approached me with the idea of creating an app. They had developed successful ones before. That's how the idea of recording my meditations and making them available came about. There was no business plan, no name, no logo—just the idea.

They started building the platform, and I began recording meditations. That's how Meditation Moments was born, and our dream team came together.

Only later did we conduct deeper research into the market, the competition, and what people wanted or were missing. The plan gradually took shape. Once half of the meditations and music were ready, we launched the app. We could have waited another year to complete all the content, but instead, we decided to move forward. And because we did, the app gained 10,000 users in its first month. Those early users gave us feedback that allowed us to continuously improve the app, tailoring it more to the needs of the audience.

Briefly, what we have covered so far: create your plan, do your research, map out your steps, gather your team, and take action as quickly as possible. Don't wait for everything to be perfect before you start—you'll never be fully ready. Just start. You don't have to be great to get started, but you do have to start to become great.

If you've done your research and are serious about your goal but still don't know exactly how to begin, my advice is simple: start, take action, and the path will reveal itself. As you move forward, you'll learn, adjust, and grow into the person who can achieve your goal.

Step 11: Do Whatever It Takes

You know your goal, and you've created a strategic plan. But in reality, things rarely go exactly as expected, and you must always be vigilant and ready to adjust your course. Every plan changes once you start putting it into action. Be prepared to steer your plan in a new direction whenever needed.

If your strategy isn't working as expected, revise it. Circumstances change, and sticking rigidly to an outdated plan can be counterproductive. The key is to anticipate and be flexible, while not abandoning your goal due to uncertainty.

I often hear people say: "My goal is A, but it's not going so well, so now I've switched to B." And not long after, they shift to goal C. Sound familiar? When you're constantly changing your goals, you lose direction, focus, and momentum. It can feel like you've been busy all day but accomplished nothing. Flexibility is crucial, but don't lose sight of your main objective. Keep your eyes on the prize, even when the path shifts.

On my sailing trips, I was entirely at the mercy of the weather. When the wind died down, I had to turn on the engine. When storms approached, I had to reduce the sail or change course.

The power of the sea and wind taught me humility, but also the importance of being ready to adapt at any moment. I learned to move with nature's forces, adjusting without losing sight of my destination.

Another notable example comes from Elon Musk's journey with SpaceX. After repeated failures and rocket crashes, he didn't abandon his goal of private space exploration. Instead, Musk and his team adjusted their approach with every setback, learning from each failure. Flexibility and perseverance kept the vision alive. Eventually, SpaceX succeeded in launching reusable rockets—something once thought impossible. Musk's ability to stay flexible while never losing sight of his ultimate goal is a powerful reminder that doing whatever it takes means staying committed, no matter the setbacks.

Flexibility is about bending and resilience. When you bend with the challenges that come your way, you won't break. Like water, which flows around obstacles, being adaptable is an incredibly powerful skill. As Lao Tzu, the ancient Chinese sage, said: *"Water is elusive. By giving a little, you can overcome the rigid edges of life. Water is soft and agile, yet it can wear down the hardest stone. Flexibility overcomes. If you are prepared to let go, resistance decreases. By being as flexible as water and prepared to appear weak, you remain calm, and evil cannot enter your heart. When you stay soft and overcome the hard, you will be indestructible. When you flow like water, you will always find your way."*

In short, the ability to adjust course without losing focus on your destination is critical. Be flexible, but don't drift aimlessly. Stay focused on your goal, adapt when necessary, and do whatever it takes to get there.

"The man who chases two rabbits catches neither."
— **Confucius**

Step 12: Focus on Your Goals

"How can I maintain focus?" is a question I'm asked repeatedly. What do you mean when you say that you lose focus? Focus is about directing your attention with precision. You can only stay focused if you have something to focus on—a clear goal. Think of it like photography: you need to aim and adjust the focus. You can't capture two different things clearly with one camera. The same goes for your life—focus on the few, not the many.

Losing focus can be disastrous. Imagine driving without paying attention to the road—you're inviting an accident. The same applies to life. When you lose your targeted attention, or focus, the consequences can be just as serious.

If your goal is clear, distractions fade into the background. But if your goal is vague, it's hard to maintain focus. If your goal is too small, even minor problems can obscure it. The sharper and more compelling your goal, the easier it is to stay on track. If you truly know what you want, and it's a goal that ignites your passion, losing focus becomes less likely.

So, stay focused on your goal. Don't let fear, criticism, or the opinions of others pull you off course. And be careful not to divide your attention too much. Multitasking is often a trap—it scatters your energy. When you're juggling too many things at once, nothing gets done as well as it could, and you lose the ability to focus. This leaves you feeling overwhelmed and unproductive. Of course, everyday life requires handling multiple tasks, but when it comes to pursuing your goal, try to focus your attention on that one thing as much as possible. The more time and attention you spend on it, the faster you'll reach your goal.

Do you want to master a new skill? Focused attention for a few hours every day will take you further, faster, than sporadic efforts. Imagine dedicating three solid hours each day to learning something specific—your results will be much better than if you just occasionally watch a tutorial or read an article. Deep learning happens when you immerse yourself, when you shut out distractions and dive into the work completely.

The same holds true if you're an entrepreneur. Someone who pours 80 hours a week working passionately and attentively will accomplish more than someone who spends 40 hours a week on their business. Input equals output. The more focused energy and time you devote, the greater your results will be.

Focused attention means making clear choices. It requires you to prioritize and manage your time effectively. As Gandalf the wizard said in *The Lord of the Rings*, "*All we have to do is decide what to do with the time that is given us.*" You have 24 hours every day, just like everyone else. So, when you say, "*I have no time,*" what you really mean is that you've allowed yourself to become overwhelmed. You think you have to do more than is humanly possible in the time available, and that drives up your stress levels.

Give some thought to what you don't really need to do. Take a step back and evaluate: What can you let go of? What unnecessary things are eating up your time? Are you spending too much time on tasks that don't align with your goals? Cut out the distractions that aren't moving you closer to your destination. And what would you do if you had more time available?

Often, we get so caught up in the busyness of life that we lose sight of the essence of our existence. So, whenever possible, do everything with undivided attention. Prioritize the tasks that matter most, and then give them your full energy. And do everything that's necessary, everything you can think of and what you could not have imagined. Do everything you have to, as long as it's legal and you don't harm others.

When you think you've done everything, keep going; there's almost always something you haven't done or thought of. Know that even in the darkest of moments, success can be within reach. "Success is on the razor's edge of failure," I learned from Dan Peña. Sometimes, when everything seems dark, you're actually closer to success than you realize. My own path to financial independence came out of what felt like a hopeless situation—burdened by enormous debt, I had no choice but to focus relentlessly on my goal. All my attention, energy, and time were poured into achieving that one thing, and eventually, I made it through.

As Jim Rohn used to say, *"Success is neither magical nor mysterious. Success is the natural consequence of consistently applying basic fundamentals."* And one of those fundamentals is focus. You can't scatter your energy and expect great results. You must keep your eyes on your goal and consistently take steps toward it every day.

Focus, focus, focus! Don't let distractions or setbacks pull you off course. Stay disciplined and stay flexible. Focus all your attention, your time, and your energy on achieving your goals. And do whatever it takes to live your best life.

The Keys to Mastering Your Mindset

- **Success is a science:** Success results from mindset and a focused strategy, combining belief in yourself with preparation, practice, and hard work.
- **Action is key:** Achieving your dreams requires not only thinking but also doing. Action brings results.
- **Create a roadmap:** To reach your goals, you need a clear, step-by-step plan outlining your actions and path.
- **Self-knowledge check:** Understand where you are now, where you want to go, and what obstacles are in your way.
- **Set clear goals:** Defining short- and long-term goals is crucial for direction and motivation.
- **Focus on what matters:** Prioritize and concentrate on key areas to avoid distractions and scattered attention.
- **Overcome fear:** Fear holds many back, but it can be managed by understanding the worst-case scenario and focusing on the facts.

- **Make decisive choices:** Indecisiveness leads to missed opportunities, while confident decision-making is key to success.
- **Practice self-discipline:** Discipline is essential for long-term success, as shortcuts don't lead to lasting results.
- **Passion fuels success:** Passion drives sustained effort, enthusiasm, and attention to detail, leading to greater achievements.
- **Persevere through challenges:** Many give up too early; perseverance is crucial in overcoming obstacles and achieving success.
- **Avoid negativity:** Negative attitudes repel opportunities, while positivity attracts people and situations that can help you succeed.
- **Address limiting beliefs:** Self-limiting thoughts create invisible barriers. Success requires breaking free from these mental constraints.
- **Ambition drives growth:** Embrace ambition and aim to grow continuously. Settling for mediocrity limits your potential.
- **Success follows discipline:** Success is built through consistent, disciplined actions, while failure comes from repeated mistakes and poor habits.
- **Use the 12-step strategy:** By following these 12 steps, you can systematically transform your dreams into reality through clear goals, focused action, and persistent effort.

Closing Words

This story is almost finished. But yours may just have started. It's time to put the theory of this book into practice and make an effort. No one else will do that for you.

Know that the results you get in your daily life are the result of your mindset and your habitual behavior. Rewrite your subconscious program. Change your thoughts, change your convictions, and change your behavior: master your mindset.

This book isn't meant to be read just once. At the very least, read it one more time; really study it. It can and will change your life. It contains virtually everything you need to give substance to your best life. If you understand what I've written down and apply it, this book can be of immeasurable value to you.

Every day brings new opportunities. Every day is the beginning of the rest of your life. Every day is an unwritten page. Imagine your life as a book and you as the writer: How do you want your story to go? Are you going to let others fill the pages? Or are you going to write your own life story?

Live your best life! Why wouldn't you? You can no longer say you don't know how. Life is largely self-created for those who believe in it.

Know that people on their deathbeds most regret that they didn't have the courage to remain true to themselves, that they lived too much according to the expectations of others, that they didn't follow their hearts enough, and that they did too little of what they really wanted to do. Many also regret having spent too much time on work and too little on the people they loved.

Imagine that at the end of this earthly existence, the movie of your life was to be played for you so you could experience it one last time. Would you want to fast-forward through it, or would you rather rewind it a few more times to continue enjoying many beautiful moments?

Once again, I ask you: What do you really want? Who do you want to be? What is in your personal statute? What are your personal values? What is your dream? What are you going to do with the rest of your life?

The End

The clock is ticking. This life has a deadline. The end is drawing nearer with each passing minute. Maybe you have 30 more summers, maybe just 1. No one knows.

Everything is in perpetual motion, everything changes, everything passes. A hundred years from now, you'll be gone. Everything you own will belong to someone else. Possessions, fame, and fortune are as fleeting as time. Your first love, unforgettable moments, memories that make you who you are: that past and the future, everything passes.

And you? How has your life moved on in the last 5, 10, 20 years? What have you done with your time? And what are you going to do with the time you have left?

This universe will probably continue to exist for millions if not billions of years, not quite long enough to call it eternal. Only love and silence are immortal. Omnia vincit amor.

Our 80 or so years on this planet are not even a flash of lightning in eternity. Enjoy your time here and have faith in the journey.

Live in the light of your own being.

Live from a place of love.

Live a meaningful life.

"Be a source of inspiration to others,
be the light in the darkness,
be the smile that dries the tears,
be a student of life and, first and foremost,
be who you are deep inside: yourself.
Surround yourself with people who believe in you,
who are honest and sincere,
people who encourage you when you are about to give up
and can help you become the best version of yourself.
Live Your Best Life."

– Michael George Pilarczyk

Sources and Literature

Allen, James (1983). *As a Man Thinketh*. Camarillo, DeVorss & Company.

Branson, Richard (2007). *Screw It, Let's Do It*. London, Virgin Books.

Chopra, Deepak (1995). *The Seven Spiritual Laws of Success*. Novato, New World Library.

Chopra, Deepak (2004). *Synchrodestiny*. London, Ebury Publishing.

Chopra, Deepak, & Tanzi, Rudolphe E. (2013). *Super Brain*. London, Ebury Publishing.

Clason, George S. (1998). *The Richest Man in Babylon*. Penguin Books.

Coelho, Paulo (2002). *The Alchemist*. London, Harper Collins UK.

Covey, Stephen R. (1989). *The 7 Habits of Highly Effective People*. New York, Simon & Schuster.

Davidji (2012). *Secrets of Meditation*. Hay House UK.

de Saint-Exupéry, Antoine (2016). *The Little Prince*. London, Pan Macmillan.

Dweck, Carol S. (2006). *Mindset: The New Psychology of Success*. New York, Ballantine Books.

Frankl, Victor E. (2006). *Man's Search for Meaning*. Boston, Beacon Press.

Garfield, Charles (1987). *Peak Performers*. New York, Avon Books.

Haanel, Charles F. (2008). *The Master Key System*. New York, Ataria Books.

Haich, Elisabeth (2000). *Initiation*. Santa Fe, Aurora Press.

Hill, Napoleon (2008). *Think and Grow Rich*. New York, Tarcher Penguin.

Hill, Napoleon (2016). *Think and Grow Rich*. Amersfoort, Invictus Publishing.

Krishnamurti (1989). *Think on These Things*. New York, Harper Perennial.

Lipton, Bruce H. (2010). *The Biology of Belief: Unleashing the Power of Consciousness, Matter, and Miracles*. New York, Hay House LLC.

Mulford, Prentice (2008). *Thoughts Are Things*. Wilder Publications.

Peña Sr., Daniel S. (1998). *Building Your Own Guthrie*. Great Western Development.

Peña Sr., Daniel S. Angus (2009). *Your First 100 Million*. Guthrie Castle Ltd.

Rinpoche, Tulku Lobsang (2008). *108 Questions from the Secret Wisdom of Tibet*. Vienna, Nangten Menlang International.

Rinpoche, Tulku Lobsang (2013). *Mindfulness in Daily Life*. Vienna, Nangten Menlang International.

Rinpoche, Tulku Lobsang (2015). *Nothing Higher than Happiness*. Banyan Centre.

Sri Sri Ravi Shankar, H.H. (2007). *Mind Matters*. Bangalore, Sri Sri Publications Trust.

Tolle, Eckhart (2008). *A New Earth*. London, Penguin Putnam Inc.

Tzu, Lao (1999). *Tao Te Ching*. London, Frances Lincoln.

Wattles, Wallace D. (2007). *The Science of Getting Rich*. Vermont, Destiny Books.

Watts, Alan (1989). *The Way of Zen*. New York, Random House/ Vintage Books.

Wilhelm, Richard (1991). *I Tjing, wAnkh-Hermes*. Deventer.

About the Author

Michael George Pilarczyk is a mindset and mindfulness teacher, author, and speaker in the fields of consciousness, self-development, leadership, meaning, spiritual growth, and personal and business success. As an expert in reprogramming thought patterns, he has helped many people experience more joy, peace, success, and happiness by breaking through limiting beliefs and fostering new insights.

From 1992 to 1999, Michael was a popular radio DJ on the number-one Dutch station, Radio 538. He also worked as a VJ and hosted TV shows on national television. After founding several companies and selling his media business in 2007, Michael took a sabbatical to pursue a lifelong dream, sailing along the Mediterranean coast for seven years. He has authored bestsellers *Dancing in Heaven* (2014), *Master Your Mindset* (2016/2025), *You Become as You Think* (2021), and *Design Your Own Life* (2023), selling over a million books.

Michael is married to Cindy Pilarczyk-Koeman. They live on Mallorca, a Spanish island in the Mediterranean Sea. Together, they are the founders of Masterminds Academy and the Meditation Moments app.

Listen to Michael's meditations: www.meditationmoments.com
Michael's website: www.mistermindset.com
Social media: @mistermindset

Write a Review

I hope *Master Your Mindset* has given you valuable insights and that you'll take action with them—because the secret is in the doing.

I'd love to read your feedback, and you'd make me very happy by leaving an online review.

Thank you! Wishing you all the best, Michael

Index